confident communication for leaders
*How to communicate with confidence.
Anywhere. Anytime. With anyone.*

confident communication for leaders

How to communicate with confidence.
Anywhere. Anytime. With anyone.

by
CAROL FOX & KATHRYN GORMAN

Published by Life Performance Books

A Division of Life Performance Pty Ltd 2017

Copyright © 2017 by Carol Fox & Kathryn Gorman

All rights reserved. No part of this publication may be reproduced, stored in a retrieval system, or transmitted in any form or by any means, electronic, mechanical, photocopying, recording or otherwise, without the prior written permission of the publisher.

First printing: 2006
Third Edition

National Library of Australia Cataloguing – in – publication data
ISBN 0 9775877 7 0

Published by Life Performance Books
P.O. Box 629
Williamstown 3016
Victoria. AUSTRALIA

www.lifeperformance.com.au

Confident Communication for Leaders – How to communicate with confidence, anywhere, anytime. With anyone.

1.Leadership 2. Personal Growth 3. NLP 4. Psychology 5. Communication

Font: Arial

Images: istock photo, pexels and author's personal collection

dedication

Many years ago, we did our initial training in hypnotherapy and Neuro Linguistic Programming (NLP). We are grateful to Pip McKay for all she taught us...and for making learning fun.

The concepts in this book stem from two key sources: the founders of NLP–Richard Bandler & John Grinder–whose transformational discoveries form the basis for some of the techniques in this book, and a notable practitioner of NLP, Dr Tad James of Advanced Neuro Dynamics.

There's a saying often attributed to Albert Einstein, but actually said by Sir Isaac Newton: *'If I have seen further, it is by standing on the shoulders of giants'*. We have been blessed with many giant teachers over the years, who have helped us learn and become confident communicators. We are grateful to them all.

what's in this book

dedication

chapter 1 **confident communication skills –**
what they are and why you need to use them

chapter 2 **keeping it real –**
how your reality determines the way you communicate

chapter 3 **how you communicate**…really

chapter 4 **the stories we tell ourselves –**
the link between the subconscious mind, comfort zones and confident communication

chapter 5 **the 4 communication preferences –**
what they are and why you need to know them

chapter 6 **visual communicators –**
how others see what you communicate

chapter 7 **auditory communicators –**
how others hear what you communicate

chapter 8 **kinesthetic communicators –**
how others experience what you communicate

chapter 9 **data digital communicators –**
how others understand what you communicate

chapter 10 **when the sh*t hits the fan –**
what can happen when these four communicators get together and what to do about it

chapter 11 **which communication preference am i?**
a quick quiz

chapter 12 **figure it out –**
identifying communication preferences and why you might want to

chapter 13 **how to speak another language –**
and why you might need to

chapter 14 **chill out –**
how to use communication to diffuse a tense situation

chapter 15 **email secrets –**
how to write the right way

chapter 16 **um, er, maybe –**
how to make fast, easy, decisions, and why you already know how to

chapter 17 **stand in their shoes –**
why you might need to do this and how to in 3 easy steps

chapter 18 **word play –**
how to use words to say what you mean and mean what you say

chapter 19 **metaprograms matter –**
what they are and why you need to use them

chapter 20 **body language bonus –**
the confidence stance

chapter 21 **how to be a confident communicator in your world**

bibliography

suggested reading

confident communication programs

about the authors

chapter 1   confident communication skills –
*what they are and
why you need to use them*

what is confident communication?

> *Communication is to a relationship
> what breathing is to life.*
> Virginia Satir (1916-1988) Psychotherapist

At a recent sporting conference, Carol, author of this book, crossed paths with a famous Australian swimmer. In fact, "famous" is not the word: a "living legend" is a more accurate description. This woman's manner was confident and warm. She introduced herself by name, rather than assuming Carol would know who she was. She smiled graciously and shook Carol's hand.

Then, to Carol's surprise, she greeted her by name, having remembered meeting Carol at a swimming event...twelve years previously. Carol was thrilled; to have one of her swimming heroes remember her made her feel incredibly special. But mostly, she reported how this woman appeared to be the ultimate "confident communicator".

"Confident" comes from the Latin ***"confidente"*** meaning ***"having full trust".*** The origin of the word ***"communication"*** is the Latin ***"communicare"*** meaning ***"to share",*** and ***"communis"*** translating as ***"common".*** Based on this, we can define confident communication as ***"sharing and finding***

things in common, in a way which creates connection and trust". The confident communicator is someone who uses innate or learned skills to do this.

Back in the mid-twentieth century, the renowned family therapist Virginia Satir said, *'Communication is to a relationship what breathing is to life'.* As dramatic as her statement looks and sounds–we need good communication as much as we need to breathe–the importance of confident communication cannot be underrated.

And if that's making things look, sound or feel stressful because you feel or think you're not good at communicating so what possible hope do you have…you might choose now to read on. Because this book contains skills to help you become a confident communicator, skills you already have inside you, skills to make confident communication as easy and natural and automatic as…breathing.

Confident communicators are aware of others and their needs. They communicate in a way which is uplifting, inclusive of others, and always favourable for all involved. Most of all they appreciate and respect different models of the world. They know that no-one on this planet, not even the most enlightened, perceives reality as it really is. Confident communicators acknowledge all realities as valid, and this respect comes through in their communication and in how they interact with others.

Confident communicators are just as warm and graceful in their interactions with someone who might be perceived as "unimportant" or "little", as they are with those who hold great importance in the eyes of the world, such as a celebrity or a president. This is the true graciousness of the confident communicator. Applying the concepts from this book in your life now, can assist your ability to communicate in a way which is sincere, gracious and confident.

who we are

We are women, teachers, athletes, advocates, writers, communicators, therapists, trainers, daughters, mothers and friends. We were not born brimming with confident communication. We had to learn it.

In some ways, this may be easier than someone who has this gift innately. For we learned what *not* to do. And we learned what works. We have used these skills to bring us new work, opportunities, friends, connections, resources and the joy and fun of happy, confident communication.

We use most of these techniques every day, or whenever we need them. If we had seen, heard and learned these skills sooner, we could have avoided a great deal of angst in life, and allowed in a lot more fun. So, we want to share them with you.

We have seen how, when we teach what works to others, their life is transformed. And that is a cool thing to observe. Simply by learning and applying a new skill, our life can change for the better. It can change for you, too…but only if that's important to you, of course.

who you are

Perhaps you are someone who does not feel at all like a confident communicator. Or possibly you already feel confident, yet want to improve. Maybe you find it difficult in social or work situations, and even the thought of communicating with a total stranger triggers anxiety inside you. Or perhaps you feel confident to do this, yet struggle to engage them in conversation…or end it elegantly. Possibly to the world you appear confident, yet inside you are shaking in your boots. Whether you were born confident, became confident or are yet to be confident, there's a reason you picked up this book: you want to learn more. And we can assist you with that.

If you've been struggling with communicating confidently, or you want to manage your skills more effectively, there are plenty of juicy and valuable skills right within this book which can help you. Because here's the thing: life can be fun and easy. And so can communication.

And identifying and applying new skills can help make it so. They can give you the edge, help you play more effectively in life and definitely help you have more fun. Some dude—we don't know who—once said, *Life was not meant to be easy.* We think that dude was a pessimist. And a party-pooper. Maybe they were weighed down by all the burdens that taking on everybody else's baggage can cause.

Whatever the case, we would like to offer this alternative: **Life was meant to be easy.** Life was meant to be fun. Life was meant to be filled with playful events and joy-filled moments and clear, confident communication. We *can* play in life, have fun and learn, and as ex-school teachers we can guarantee you this: *learning can and IS fun.* If you don't believe us, go and watch small children playing. If you don't have any children in your home or your life, then have a good look next time you pass a local primary school or playground. (Don't loiter too long though; stranger, danger and all that. #*awkward*) If you need to, Google "Children having fun playing".

Our point is, when you watch children play, they just have fun. They engage, they laugh, they ponder, they communicate, they fascinate. They observe and learn and if they don't know how to do something, they figure it out. This is how we are meant to move through life: with playful curiosity. With awe. And with joy.

Anything else means we've simply wandered off the right track. And everyone knows that it's easy to get back onto the right track, the fast track, the best track: just take one simple step. And then another. And keep on going.

So, if you want to read a book that is long and complex and reads like a technical thesis, then perhaps this is not the book for you. We suggest you put it down and step away from the information. However, if you want to open yourself to the possibility that confident communication can be fun and easy, structured and simple, then you can open yourself now to see, hear, receive and process valuable information which could even, possibly, change your life for the better now. Only if that's important to you, of course.

why you need confident communication skills

Communication skills are skills which help you better see, hear and understand who you are, how you gather data and what you do with that when you communicate. Confident communication skills are skills to help arm yourself for work and play, play the game, deter obstacles and navigate your way to your next destination. They help you achieve what you want in life.

The purpose of this book is to create even more awareness about you and others and how we all communicate. This book includes practical information which is:

- ✓ easy to apply
- ✓ fun and simple
- ✓ saves you time
- ✓ gets powerful results

In our experience as practitioners, and presenters, we believe the following three statements are true about being a confident communicator:

- Do the same thing; you'll get the same result.
- Success is a pattern and patterns can be learned.
- Every individual has the resources they need to succeed.

These three principles form the basis of communicating confidently so you can help yourself and others anywhere, anytime. When we increase our understanding of other people, it allows us to accept the differences that exist, rather than judging, criticising and making them wrong. This understanding ultimately leads to creating a better world to live in, and to crystal-clear, confident communication.

confident communication skills do _NOT_:
- work...if you don't use them
- make every single problem in your life magically disappear—only *you* can do that.
- disconnect you from those who are important to you
- disempower you in any way, shape or form

confident communication skills _DO_ help you to:
- happily and effectively manage your life
- network easily and effortlessly
- maintain happy relationships
- create your life the way you want
- make good things happen
- attract fun, fantastic, fabulous friends & curious, calm, clever colleagues and clients
- help yourself and others
- fill your life with love, joy, peace
- stay empowered

So, go ahead. Use them. Read on.

But only if these things are important to you of course

chapter 2   keeping it real –
how your reality determines
the way you communicate

what if we never perceive what's real...

Mihaly Csikszentmihalyi, a Hungarian Psychologist speaks in his book *Flow: The Psychology of Optimal Experience* of how you gather information from the world. Out of approximately two million bits of information surrounding you, you are only *consciously* aware of around 134 bits per second (bps).

At every moment, you are literally inundated at both a conscious and subconscious level with information. Imagine going to the supermarket. You walk into the store and you are surrounded by external stimuli such as signs, colour, noises, pricing and your body responds. Perhaps your heart beats a bit faster, the sound of a crying child disturbs you, you feel warm or cool, you have self-talk reminding you to buy milk, or you mentally add up the cost of your groceries as you push your trolley around the store. If we had to consciously be aware of everything we can see, taste, touch, smell and feel and pay attention to it all we would be in overwhelm. So, we have a filter called the Reticular Activating System (RAS), which filters most of this information for us. Consequently, we are only aware of a small piece of the actual reality occurring around us.

Some of us pay more attention to what we see, some to what we hear, some of us are more aware of how things feel and some of us pay more attention to data, facts and figures. Then, based on this small amount of information, and the information we already have stored in our mind, we create what is referred to in the field of Neuro Linguistic Programming (NLP) as our Model of the World.

What this means is that **_none of us_ perceive reality as it really is.** We only perceive around 134 "bits" of reality per second. We **all** have a different perception of reality. This explains why ten different witnesses at an accident scene can have ten different experiences of what has occurred, based on what they have seen, heard, felt and calculated.

You may have seen this footage on YouTube: Daniel Simons of University of Illinois, and Christopher Chabris of Harvard University conducted a study demonstrating how much we can delete information. In their study, subjects were asked to watch video footage of people throwing a basketball back & forth. The viewer was asked to focus and count how many times the basketball was passed.

In the middle of the video clip a man dressed in a gorilla suit moves through the middle of the game and then out of sight again. When asked, an average of 50% of the subjects didn't see the gorilla pass through the game!

Why? Well, for some people they were focusing so much on the counting and data, that they missed out on the visual detail of the gorilla.

my model of the world

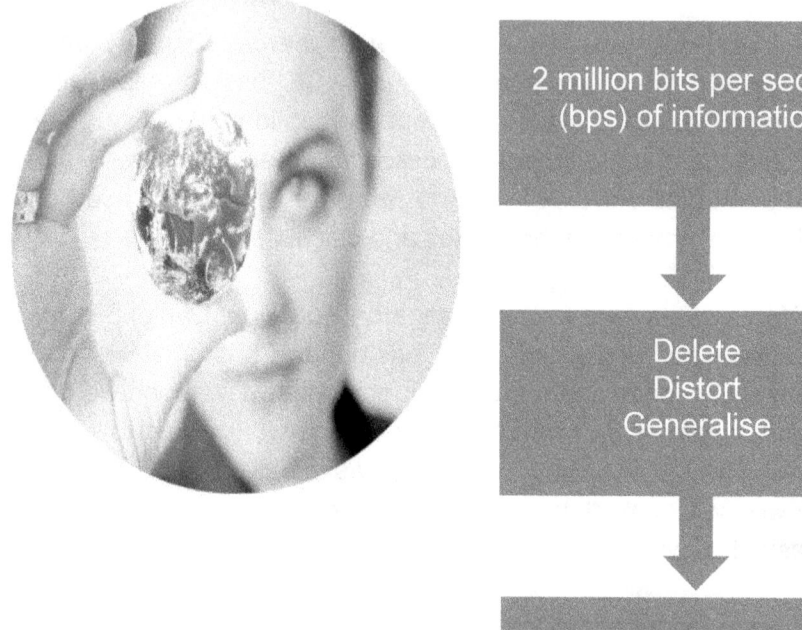

Our "reality" can be as small as .000067%* of a total possibility*

Flow: The Psychology of Optimal Experience by Mihaly Csikszentmihaly

imagine going to visit a friend...
Some people will enter their friend's home and immediately look around and check out all the things they can see. Some people will hear the music playing in the background or pay attention to background sounds such as traffic or birds. Some people will get a feel for the place and pick up on the good or bad vibes in the home. Others will ask questions about the place. For example, *'How old is it? How large is the land? How much did you pay for it?'* Depending on our filters, we will perceive or delete particular pieces of information.

If two people visit the same home, they can come away with very different perceptions of it. This often happens with couples. One might say *'Did you see that amazing new pond in the back yard?'* And the other might reply, *'No, I didn't notice that. But did you feel the bad vibes when we walked in? Do you reckon John and Sally are happy together?'* The first person might reply, *'How could you not see the fish pond? It was huge! And what do you mean, "Are they happy?" They were smiling, weren't they?'*

In this situation, the first person has paid more attention to what they have <u>seen</u> and the second to what they have <u>felt</u>. **Both of them are right.** They have just picked up on different parts of the reality occurring all around them.

In the nineteenth century, the German Philosopher Friedrich Nietzsche wisely observed, *'You have your way. I have my way. As for the right way, the correct way, and the only way, it does not exist.'* We are programmed from birth to perceive and then defend our concept of reality. But that does not always make us an effective or confident communicator.

As we gather information from the world, our mind will **delete**, **distort** and **generalise** information based on the beliefs we hold internally. If someone believes they are stupid, their mind may **delete** from their experience any time they do something that is clever. Their mind will **distort** information, so if someone says to them *'You are so clever'*, they may hear a sarcastic tone where there is none. Their mind will **generalise** their experiences to support the belief they are stupid, so they continue to create incidents, such as consistently failing exams, in order to support their theory.

Of course, this is all subconscious. None of us would want this consciously. It's human nature to want to be happy and successful. Yet the subconscious mind is so powerful that it controls and runs programs automatically for us, sometimes even programs that give us a result we don't consciously want.

The deletion of information also has an impact on how we communicate with other people. Whenever we judge someone, or have negative opinions about someone or something, we tend to justify our own reality and make that person wrong. We effectively delete anything good about them from our reality. In this situation, if we want confident and effective communication, we can use a simple tool called a **"reframe"**.

A "reframe" offers us a different view of the picture. It makes things sound and feel clearer and it opens us to new information, valuable information we may have been discarding. With our new information, we can more confidently communicate our message. We can be seen, heard, received and understood, which in turn gifts us with more confidence. It's a viciously brilliant cycle.

how "reframing" helped us

Carol woke up one morning feeling flat, fluey, shaky and incredibly nervous. She would have preferred to stay in bed, but she was on Day One of a three-day conference, at which she was a keynote speaker. She had no choice but to get out of bed and perform. She knew she needed to reframe her perception of the day, and of herself. So, she used the reframe tool we are about to share with you, and could greet the day at peak performance.

Other days she may wake up feeling flat, but if she has a quiet day where she can take it easy, she does not apply the reframe tool. It's not needed. Plus, she knows it's also important to listen to your body and honour its needs.

This reframe tool is not needed by everyone. Some people might not see, get or understand why you need to reframe. They are what we call "glass-half-full" people and their mind will naturally reframe negative experiences for them. You may have heard the term glass-half-empty? People who think this way find the reframe tool immensely valuable. We'll talk more about this when we discuss the motivation metaprogram.

how "reframing" helped others

One of our clients—we'll call him Ron—recently asked us to come and assess his "Lazy Team". When we got there, we observed the team, as Ron pointed out all the "lazy" behaviours of the team. We saw happy, efficient workers making calls, taking orders, making appointments, printing out successful programs. Their workplace was a hive of activity and industriousness. Yet, Ron was so busy concentrating on his perception of reality—that his team were lazy—he deleted their productive behaviour...the behaviour we could clearly see. He distorted how long they were taking breaks and he made generalisations from the few "lazy" behaviours which he saw occurring.

At one point, he made the comment, 'See that woman there? June? She just went to the toilet to get out of work. She was there for ten minutes. She's so lazy'. Carol's reply was, 'Wow, that's interesting. I actually saw her get up and go, and she was only in the toilet for a few minutes'. Because of his belief in his own reality, this manager even distorted time to make his reality the right one.

After explaining the impact of thinking this way, we asked Ron if it was worthwhile having a different viewpoint. He conceded it could be, so we asked him, 'What are seven good things about your team?' He was quiet for a full minute, struggling to elicit one positive thing about his team. (This is how immersed in his reality he was.)

Eventually, he offered, 'They dress professionally'. When prompted, it became easier and easier as he began to focus his awareness on the possibility that maybe there were things his team actually did right.

When we consider that around 93% of our communication is at a subconscious mind level, imagine the impact of his body language when he began to focus on the good things about his team. He wondered why they were suddenly more motivated. They were responding to his positive body language now, rather than the un-motivating energy draining, distrusting body language of old.

It was important for Ron and his staff, and of course the success of his company, that we could highlight a different reality for him by using a **reframe tool**. This enabled him to effectively "reframe" the experience he was having with his team. Incidentally, as we left the building, one of the staff members pulled us aside. She thanked us for what we had done, saying she could see and feel a shift in him already. *#happy outcome*

how a reframe can help you

Whenever you are feeling negative about yourself, another person, or a situation, a useful tool to have is the **"reframe tool"**. This technique allows you to conveniently and quickly change your current reality, through focussing on the positives in a situation rather than the negatives. Of course, it's not the only way to reframe, but it is one of the fastest and most effective we've successfully used.

how to reframe

Think of a person or situation you are negative about, one you want to change, and ask yourself the following:

Around a **person**, ask yourself:
"What are seven good things about that person?"

Around a **situation**, ask yourself:
"What are seven good things about this situation?"

Around **yourself**, ask:
"What are seven good things about myself?"

Accept the first things which come into your mind – this is your subconscious mind communicating with you. Much like a search engine, it is trained to answer questions.

Sometimes, if a situation is loaded with emotion, it's possible you may need a few moments to focus yourself in on the positives. Just ask yourself the question, then note whatever pops into your head or the images your mind gives you, or the feelings or data you are presented with.

Ron saw an image of his staff being professionally-dressed, and although, this may have seemed trivial in the scheme of his complaints, accepting this got the ball rolling for him, so to speak, enabling him to identify more positive things about his team. This is the way your subconscious mind communicates with you, so accept whatever it gives you, no matter how silly, irrelevant or even ludicrous it seems.

Last week, Carol did this exercise with a woman who was reframing her boss's behaviour. The woman confided that she hated her boss so much, the only good thing she could say about him was "he is resigning soon". Carol accepted that, wrote it down and this acceptance triggered some more positive observations, which helped this client shift her perception of reality, and thus her communication. This is the effectiveness of reframing.

A few years ago, the motivational author Dr. Wayne Dyer stated, *"Loving people live in a loving world. Hostile people live in a hostile world. But it's the same world. How come?"*

It's possible the answer is...our perception of reality.

inspirational reframing

Have you heard of Jim MacLaren? At twenty-one, he graduated from Yale, a scholar, promising actor, and a 6'5" (198cm), three hundred pound (136 kilogram) defensive lineman. At twenty-two, Jim was hit by a New York City bus, thrown some eighty feet, pronounced dead on arrival at Bellevue Hospital. After 18 hours of surgery, his life was stabilized.

Thirteen days after waking from a coma, he began a gruelling, three-month rehabilitation. The doctors told him that there was no medical reason he should be alive and that he'd be in a hospital bed for six months. In addition to the numerous internal injuries, Jim lost his left leg eight inches below the knee.

Some people who lose a leg may become depressed or very inward focused. This is a completely understandable reaction to such a traumatic event. Jim MacLaren decided that he'd do something significant with his situation. He was inspired by an event called the *Hawaiian Ironman*, which involves a 2.4 mile (3.8 kilometre) swim, a 112 mile (180 kilometre) bike ride, followed by a 26.2 mile (42 kilometre) marathon, all completed in one day. Acquiring a prosthetic, Jim trained for this event, and went on to compete in the Hawaiian Ironman. This race is hard enough for able-bodied athletes, let alone someone who has a prosthetic limb, placing incredible strain on his functioning leg.

He continued to compete in the Iron Man event against many able-bodied athletes, feeling happy and proud with his accomplishments. Other athletes were inspired by his courage and achievements. Pushing himself to see what his body could do, Jim competed for seven years, aquiring the record as the fastest amputee marathon runner and triathlete in the world. He holds the Hawaii Ironman record for an amputee, with a time of 10 hours, 42 minutes. He often finished in the top third of able-bodied athletes and was inducted into the Ironman Hall of Fame.

In 1993 he participated in an Iron Man Event in California, and during the race, a van appeared unexpectedly, and Jim was knocked from his bike. He was then diagnosed as a quadriplegic.

Everything had to be done for him. He had to be fed, clothed, pulled up out of bed, even his bowels needed to be cleaned by someone else every day. Jim couldn't do anything for himself except talk. Yet Jim continued to reframe his reality. Because the injury to his spinal cord was incomplete, he regained partial use of his limbs and independence. Even though he has experienced these challenges in life, he still continues to get out of bed every day and see the positive in life. He manages to live a life which inspires other people. This is what he says about choice:

As a human being you have two choices as to how you view the events of your life: Either you can believe every act is random, or you can believe every act occurs for a reason. But what if you believe every act occurs for a reason and then hideous, unspeakable things happen to you? Well, you're faced with two choices once more. You can either believe you were cursed, or you can believe that you were somehow blessed.

With his attitude, Jim MacLaren decided that he is blessed. And if Jim MacLaren can successfully reframe himself to such success, it's possible we all can. Jim passed away in 2010, having motivated and inspired thousands, and he left a large legacy.

how reframing helps you communicate confidently

Remember the story of Ron, our client with the "lazy team"? When he reframed his team, and began to focus on the positives, this impacted on his body language, and allowed him to communicate in a way which was respectful and sincere. This is what confident communication is about.

It's normal that we don't like everyone we meet. It's normal that we have strong connections with some people, and feel little or no connection with others.

If someone we don't automatically connect with happens to be someone we work with, or for some reason we need to have good communication, then this tool can help you maintain clear and confident communication, so you can get the job done.

…With a family member or a social situation, it enables us to manage a potentially uncomfortable situation, ensuring the best outcome for all. Further, it helps us understand why people might behave the way they do. It increases our empathy, and our ability to communicate clear boundaries as needed.

In the next chapter, we will talk about the power of rapport and it's possible you will notice, hear and learn how important your self-talk and acceptance of differences are in relation to confidently communicating with others.

chapter 3   how you communicate…really

Consider this transcript from a naval radio exchange.

RADIO ONE: *Please divert your course 15 degrees to the south to avoid a collision.*

RADIO TWO: *Recommend you divert your course 15 degrees to the north to avoid a collision.*

RADIO ONE: *Negative. You will have to divert your course 15 degrees to the south to avoid a collision.*

RADIO TWO: *This is the captain of a Navy ship. I say again, divert YOUR course.*

RADIO ONE: *No, I say again, you divert YOUR course.*

RADIO TWO: *This is the Aircraft Carrier Delta, the second largest ship in our fleet. We are accompanied by three destroyers, three cruisers and numerous support vessels. I DEMAND that you change your course 15 degrees north. I say again, that's one-five degrees north, or counter measures will be undertaken to ensure the safety of this ship.*

RADIO ONE: *This is a lighthouse. Your call.*

Have you ever had a scenario in life where you've been so sure *you* are right, yet another person has been so sure *they* are right that no one wins? It's possible there was a win-win solution all along. So how can we open the communication channels and create an easy win-win? We can do this through gaining rapport.

nobody loves me, everybody hates, me think I'll go eat worms…

…You might remember this song from when you were a kid. You may have had times where you looked, sounded or felt out-of-synch with everything and everyone. And maybe you grew up and still feel this way…even some of the time. Have you ever had a situation in which you felt misunderstood? Or one where someone did not see who you really are, or, worse, saw the wrong image of you? Maybe you've felt as if no-one considers your feelings, even though you always consider theirs. Has it ever sounded as if people were not hearing you, or not listening, that your voice did not matter?

These experiences—and all human beings have had them—can cause us to feel angry, sad, disconnected, invalidated and unconfident. They can affect the way we interact in our world. They can lose us relationships and homes and jobs. They can send us on a downward spiral.

But there are solutions, and our communication skills are significant in finding them. One of the key solutions is hidden within that strange-sounding French word which you may or may not have heard of called…rapport. (pronounced ruh-por)

what is rapport?

Rapport can be defined as *"a harmonious relationship between people or groups, in which clear communication is evident".* It comes from the French word, *"rapporter"* which means *"to bring back".*

In the French language, the word rapport is used in the way English speakers use the word "relationship". In a business environment, many people are reluctant to use the word "relationship" when speaking of communication. Yet that is precisely what it is–a relationship between two people or a group of people…a rapport.

We may hesitate to communicate with our colleagues or boss in the same way that we might to our partner, children or friends. We may feel less free to be honest, direct and clear. It's why many communicators–even good ones–find a lack of poor communication in the workplace distressing. Different guidelines for communicating seem to apply to work than they do in our personal lives. And many of us may be unsure what the rules are.

Confident communicators hold the answers. They know how to develop and maintain positive, rapport-filled relationships. They know the rules. They know the tools. And you can too.

Rapport is _**not**_ about trying to make people like you, so you can get something you want. That's called manipulation.

Rapport is about having people <u>feel they are like you</u> in some way. Rapport is the ability to enter someone else's world, to make them feel you are similar, you understand them, and that you have a common bond.

The more you do this, the more flexible you can be in situations, and the more flexible you can be in situations, the greater your chances of seeing, hearing or getting information to create a win-win through confident communication.

Rapport is the ultimate tool for producing results with other people. It makes almost any task simpler, easier and more enjoyable, because when people like us they learn faster and remember more, so we get faster, more effective results.

how does this rapport thing work?

The science of body language has shown that when we like someone and are comfortable with them, we naturally align our body language with theirs. This includes our gestures, posture, facial expressions and even blinking. This is known as *"mirroring"* and when we do this with someone, we are known to be **"in rapport"**.

We will fold our arms, or cross our legs, nod, tilt our heads, back, even mirror someone's facial expressions such as smiling or frowning or wrinkling our nose. Researchers have recorded footage of people in rapport mirroring body language, and have discovered that we even *blink* in rapport!

how gaining and maintain rapport helped us

Carol was working with an AFL football team. The players were seated around their board room table, enjoying the seminar, happily in rapport with each other and their presenter. They were also in peak learning state.

The problem was that their CEO kept dropping in to visit, effectively disrupting the flow of the seminar. Furthermore, when he entered the room he would seat himself at the table, then sit back, hands enlaced on the back of his neck, arms bent at the elbows in the body language gesture we like to call the "puffed up peacock".

We have seen this gesture on many an occasion, when a male colleague has felt threatened or out of his depth. It's a peculiarly male gesture, similar to the techniques male animals use in the wild to appear larger and more powerful, to alert and disperse their perceived enemies. It is a deeply subconscious gesture and most males are consciously unaware when they are using it. Given the powerful message it communicates, females tend to notice it immediately.

Carol noted the CEO's behaviour and she also noticed how the team members behaved differently when the CEO was in the room. Several mirrored his body language, and one began making inappropriate comments in a bid, we suspect, to impress the CEO. This man was a person of influence in the player's life and they were responding to his behaviour.

Carol knew she needed to do something, and quickly, before her efforts to inspire this team was interrupted. Knowing the power of rapport, she began to mirror the body language of the CEO. As it would have looked odd for her to stand at the front of the room with her arms behind her head, she modified the gesture, mirroring his action with only one arm.

Seated at the back of the room, Kathryn observed her action, at first finding it bizarre. Then realising Carol was mirroring the CEO, Kathryn stifled a giggle. She watched on in fascination, as Carol brought her hand down. The CEO tossed Carol an odd look, then adjusted his body language, placing his hands on the boardroom table and appearing slightly bewildered. Carol continued to place herself in rapport with the CEO, matching his body language, and including him in the conversation. The players reverted to their happy rapport and peak learning state. Carol resumed the training and the team learned what they were there to learn.

how gaining and maintaining rapport helps others

Carol taught a recent seminar on '*5 things I wish I knew before joining a board*'. She included the power of rapport in her talk. Linh, one of the participants, was having difficulty communicating with another member of a board she was on. She emailed this message:

Carol, thank you so much for your recent speech about '5 things I wish I knew before joining a board'. I was intrigued by your topic as I always seem to be out of rapport with our current Chair. He does not seem to listen to me or take what I say seriously. He cuts me off when I am speaking which makes me look stupid in front of everyone. I know I have value to offer but he was not seeing who I am.

I applied the skills of rapport you taught us, and the results were miraculous! Within two minutes of the meeting beginning, he asked me my opinion on a hot topic. He has never done this before. When I spoke, he listened carefully, then thanked me. He has never done that before, either! I was able to bring other points to the table and he heard them, and we had an amiable discussion. After the meeting, he pulled me aside and thanked me for my valuable contribution. He was like a completely different man!

I am so grateful to have learned this skill. Thank you so much

*Kind regards,
Linh*

how gaining and maintaining rapport helps you

Rapport gives you a connection with someone. It gets you noticed. In a networking situation, you will be the person other people remember. In a social situation, you will be the host or guest who is full of grace and charm. In personal relationships, it gives you the ability to dodge drama and maintain connections. It helps you avoid that horrible outcome of poor communication, those unnecessary and completely avoidable misunderstandings, which can lead to breakages, breakdowns and break ups.

how do you gain and maintain rapport?
Follow these 3 steps:
1. **Observe:** Become an observer of human behaviour. You can easily master this in an hour or an afternoon because your subconscious mind already knows how to do this.

You naturally mirror people every day. You are already an expert. Watch how people behave. Observe two people communicating. Notice how they both cross their arms, or tilt their heads or nod their heads in time.

Or, observe interactions which seem not as harmonious. Note how their body language is mismatched, perhaps one has their arms folded and the other is open. Or maybe one is leaning forward and the other backwards. Watch interactions in your workplace, court, arena and living room, in reel life and in real life. Notice how obvious it is now you've become consciously aware of this thing we all do every day.

2 **Do:** When engaged in conversation, make yourself consciously mirror the other person's body language. It may feel or sound strange. You may think that it looks ridiculous or obvious. Do it anyway.

In our experience, most people will never see, feel or think you are doing anything unusual. Instead, they will see, feel or think of you as a confident communicator and a seriously cool person. They will like you. They will like you because they perceive you are like them. You're part of their tribe. You belong now. And you do.

3. **Practice:** Consciously practice mirroring people, anywhere, anytime. Practice until it becomes innate, until you find yourself in a social situation now where you magically become consciously aware of how you and someone else are completely in rapport.

Almost as if you planned it.

when to use mirroring for confident communication

When we are teaching the skill of mirroring in our workshops, we ask the audience to find a partner. They identify themselves as the storyteller or the listener. Half of the group–the listeners–are sent outside the room, where they are secretly instructed to "mirror" their partner's body language as they tell their story.

They receive an explanation of the difference between *"copying"* and *"mirroring"*. Copying comes from ego or "headspace"–it's what kids do to tease each other. Mirroring comes from a "heart-space" and gives the message that you are listening and caring. Participants are asked to go back into the room with that intent, and to listen to their partner's story whilst mirroring their body language and gestures as appropriate.

When they return to the room, their partner, the storyteller commences recounting a story they have prepared. During this exercise, the experience for most participants is a positive. The storytellers are delighted with the avid listening skills of their companions. The listeners are delighted to learn and practise one of the secrets of confident communicators. The energy generated in the room is high, fun, often filled with laughter and happy interactions. It is usually difficult to get people to stop talking.

Next, the storytellers are taken outside and asked *'Did you feel like you were being listened to? Did they look interested in your story?'* If the exercise is done properly, the majority of the participants respond with an enthusiastic *'Yes!'* When they are informed they were being "mirrored" most are extremely surprised and sometimes incredulous. They learn that this is what they do naturally with someone they like.

They are then instructed to return to their partner and mirror their body language (with a warning their partner is usually sitting in an awkward position as they know what they are up to). After thirty seconds we give them a signal to slowly and subtly **"break rapport".** This means changing their body language so they are *not* reflecting how their partner is sitting or moving. If their partner has legs crossed, they uncross their own. If their partner's head is upright, they tilt theirs. If their partner is slouched in their chair, they sit straight and tall in their own. If their partner is making excessive gestures, they make minimal movements.

As facilitators, every single time we observe this exercise, at the point when rapport is broken, the energy in the room drops dramatically. People quickly wind up their story or stop talking altogether, and they look at us to rescue them from an awkward situation.

We then ask the participants what happened and what was different. They usually say something like:

I felt like he wasn't listening, so I stopped.
The flow of the conversation stopped dead.
She was interested and then she wasn't.

When asked how that made them feel, they often report,

I felt let down, embarrassed, stupid.
Disappointed.
I felt unimportant, as if what I had to say didn't matter.

There are times when participants are unsure as to what has occurred. They just know that "something wasn't quite right". When we inform them that their partner was asked to "break rapport" with them and that's what they did, their usual response is, *'I knew he was up to something, but I couldn't pinpoint exactly what!'*

During this exercise, we often get asked, a brilliant and valid question: ***'Isn't this manipulation?'*** Participants will often comment, 'I couldn't possibly mirror someone consciously. I would feel like I was manipulating someone.'

Our response is this: **you mirror people's body language all the time!** You mirror people you like. You mirror people you are comfortable with. You mirror people you find interesting or fascinating or cool. The people in your life with whom you have a connection, are those you naturally mirror without even thinking about it consciously. You already do this.

The most important thing in mirroring someone for the purposes of increasing communication is your **intent**. If your intent is to control and manipulate someone, this is what you will communicate, and people will perceive this on some level. If your intent is to help others, build stronger connections, and have greater harmony in your workplace and your home, then you can create this through mirroring.

what happens when we come across someone whom we don't like or don't understand?

If we don't feel an instant or natural connection to someone, our body language will be out of rapport with them. If this is the case, use the **"Reframe Tool"** to find some good things about that person. This will shift your perception of them at a subconscious level. This will impact on your body language, then it's possible you will find yourself automatically aligning your body language with theirs.

If not, consciously apply the tool of mirroring to place you back in rapport, and this will open the channels for confident communication.

breaking rapport – when you might need to do this

There are times when you may choose to use your knowledge of mirroring to consciously "break rapport" with someone. This involves consciously mis-matching someone's body language.

For example, if they crossed their arms, you would uncross yours. If their legs were uncrossed, you would cross yours. Again, we do this automatically with people we are uncomfortable with or are unlike.

Some situations require you to break rapport. They may include if someone is draining your energy, if you feel their energy is invasive or overly demanding, or even if, in a social situation, someone is expressing an unwelcome interest in you...aka, "hitting on you" when you are not interested or available. We've even known clients to use this skill in work situations where they were experiencing sexual harassment. It can work like a charm.

You can also use this technique during meetings which have gone over time. It's an elegant way of communicating the meeting is over–perfect for colleagues who are known for dragging out meetings. We've found it helpful to consciously mirror the person again as we are walking out the door. It places us back in rapport, and leaves them with a confident and harmonious last impression.

If you find yourself in a situation where you are uncomfortable with someone, where their energy is overpowering or extremely negative, and they are not open to connecting, then "breaking rapport" is the perfect way to elegantly set a boundary. You don't even need to explain; you can simply excuse yourself and move away. This can be done in a respectful and caring way, remembering we all have different perspectives of reality. There are however, some realities you may choose to disassociate from, and this is a completely valid choice.

93% of communication is at a subconscious mind level

There are many statistics available on communicating and body language. Although the figures may vary slightly, the concept remains the same: a very large percentage of our communication is at a subconscious mind level.

In his book, *Kinesics & Context*, Ray L Birdwhistell states that 93% of what we communicate is done at a level that we are not even aware of. Only 7% of what we communicate is done through the actual words we use.

Of that 93%, around **55% is communicated through body language,** such as our posture, gestures, facial expressions, and even the way we dress. **38% is communicated** through the speed, volume, pauses, and tone of our **voice**. To illustrate this and hear and understand how we communicate through our tone of voice, do this. (We suggest you find a quiet place where no-one can hear you.) Repeat the below sentence seven times aloud and emphasise the underlined word:

<u>I</u> never said I would do it.

*I <u>**never**</u> said I would do it.*

*I never <u>**said**</u> I would do it.*

I never said <u>I</u> would do it.

*I never said I <u>**would**</u> do it.*

*I never said I would <u>**do**</u> it.*

*I never said I would do <u>**it**</u>.*

Seven words, one sentence, Seven different meanings.

chapter 4 the stories we tell ourselves –
the link between the subconscious mind, comfort zones and confident communication

imagine this

Imagine if it was true that in your subconscious mind every experience from the day you were born is recorded, similar to a computer hard drive. Every experience, be it positive or negative, is stored in your subconscious mind. So, everything that you've ever seen, heard, felt and thought is stored there

The interesting thing about this is, if we all have our specific experiences stored in our subconscious mind, then we are all unique. It follows, then, that no one in the world has exactly the same subconscious mind. Even identical twins, who have shared so many similar life experiences, have a different subconscious mind, as their perception of situations is unique. They may find themselves in many of the same situations, yet their perspectives will differ because their subconscious mind differs. So, no-one on the planet has an identical subconscious mind. We are all unique and the filter through which we perceive the world is unique.

If this is true, then consider this question: *Can we ever know 100% with certainty what is going on in someone else's mind?* The answer is of course "no". We can't possibly know what is going on for someone else, because we don't know what experiences they have had that may shape and influence the way they perceive the world. Yet, we have met people (and you might know someone like this) who consistently make up stories inside their own minds...thinking that they know what is going on another person's mind. This is known as a *"mind read"*.

more about the "mind read"

Remember back to the days when you were a teenager (unless you are still one, then congrats on reading this book...carry on!) and you'd be at a party or pub and you'd see someone whom you liked? What did you do? Did you go up to them and ask that person a question, engage them in cool conversation? Or did you eye them from a distance, whilst telling yourself a story about why you could not approach them?

Sadly, we have learned that most people run a story through their head to sustain their inaction. It looks and sounds something like this:

If I go up to them, they will tell me to get lost.
If I go up to them, they'll ignore me.
If I go up to them, they will laugh at me
If I go up to them, other people will make fun of me.
If I go up to them, and ask them to dance, they will say no.

Now, for you, a fear of approaching another human being with a desire to communicate may have been based on a negative real-life experience. If that's the case, we say, *'Kudos for being brave. So sorry that happened to you.'*

But in most instances, people tell us they've had no personal experience of being rejected. They may have watched others being rejected. They may have even watched others being accepted. Regardless, they created negative stories in their head, and these stories stopped them from doing what they wanted to do: meet someone new, make a new friend, hook-up.

So, why does it matter what happened as a teenager? How does that affect us now? The problem with self-stories is they can be like self-sabotage. They can stop us from doing something we want to do to get something we want. These negative stories we may be telling ourselves can prevent us from meeting new people or creating new opportunities.

Years ago, when we explained this concept of storytelling to a group of clients, one of the participants, a printer salesperson, told us a story. He recounted how he was driving past a building near his work, and saw a new business moving in. He noticed them take all their new equipment into the office building. He didn't see a photocopier, so he thought, *'Oh, I might go in and actually give them my card, and maybe sell them a photocopier.'*

Instead of doing this, he told himself a story: *'I won't go in and give them my card because they'll probably just tell me to get lost.'* Two days later, he saw his major competitor walking in with a new printer. He'd missed an opportunity because he "mind read" them, telling himself a story about how they would react. Yet the reality was that he had no idea what they would do.

do we ever really know?

In the past, we may have created these stories and assumed that we knew how someone was going to react. **The reality is we never, ever know how someone is going to react to something.** Sure, we can predict the behaviour of people we know well, yet one of the great things about being human is that we are all unique and we can change our mind at any time.

How many times have you looked at someone and thought that they were angry or worried, yet when you've asked, *'Are you okay?',* they've actually said: *'Yeah, I'm fine. I was just deep in thought'.* A few years ago, an hilarious meme travelled around the net, describing this exact phenomenon, and bringing a new phrase into our vernacular. It was "resting bitchy face" otherwise known as "RBF". Wikipedia defines it as *'a facial expression which unintentionally appears as if a person is angry, annoyed, irritated, or contemptuous, particularly when the individual is relaxed or not particularly expressing an emotion'.* It has been studied by psychologists, fascinated by the implications of this confusing mixed message which causes people the world over to "mind-read". It's worth checking out on YouTube.

Our clients sometimes talk to us about wanting a pay rise. They'll say, *'I won't ask my boss for a pay rise because if I do, she'll yell at me or tell me I don't deserve it, or she'll say no.'*

In a recent coaching session, one of Carol's clients, we will call her Annie, spent ten minutes telling Carol how nasty and mean her manager is because she wouldn't give Annie a pay rise. Turns out, Annie had never actually gone in there and asked for one in the first place. Instead, what she had done is blame her manager, and yet she hadn't even given them the chance to hear her, let alone increase her salary.

This is what is referred to in psychology as *"blame" versus "responsibility"*. It's about being **responsible** for what we need in life, rather than **blaming** another person. So, if you hear yourself making an excuse and not asking for something you want, it's possible you will recognise it as a story. Instead of creating a fairy tale about what *might* happen, you could choose to create a good story, so you get the results you want now. And who knows, it's possible you may even live happily ever after.

how stories affect public speaking performance

One of the key areas in which our clients want to communicate confidently is when public speaking is required. This could include speaking to a large room of people, or an arena, or it might be engaging within a smaller group such as a board meeting, AGM or even a regular team meeting.

When we ask an audience, *'Who has a fear of speaking in public? Do you remember the time when you stopped speaking in public, or became afraid of speaking in public?* it's usually early in life that their fear developed. It might have been when you answered a teacher's question and classmates laughed at you.

It could even be from earlier in life, answering questions from an adoring family audience in which their laughter at how cute you were was distorted, misinterpreted as being laughed at or made wrong. So many people stop speaking in public because they associate it with being ridiculed.

We often ask our audiences, '**Who here has a bad story about public speaking? Who has got a picture in their head about all the horrible things that can happen?'** and nearly everyone puts their hand up. It usually looks and sounds something like this:

I'm going to trip on the stage stairs.
The microphone will screech with feedback.
I'm going to drop my notes on the floor.
People are going to laugh at me.
People are going to be bored or fall asleep.
People are going to walk out.

Many people have pictures in their head of the horrible things that are going to happen, when in reality most people in an audience want to hear what you have to say.

how to get over a fear of speaking in public

Create a new picture in your head. Tell yourself a new story. Stop listening to the stories which keep you somewhere you don't want to be.

We ask our audience to create a new picture, a picture of what they want their experience to be, one in which their audience adores them, thinks they're wonderful and are interested in what they're going to say. It sounds and looks something like this:

The audience are here to learn something from me.
The audience values what I say.
The audience are interested in my message.
The audience applauds me at the end because they are so happy they learned something of value.

Once they start thinking about that picture, and telling themselves those stories, when they step up to speak, it's significantly easier. We all have the choice between the bad pictures and the good ones; between the bad feelings and the good feelings.

If you want to learn more about removing anxiety around public speaking, visit Carol Fox & Co. www.carolfox.com.au

how this relates to confident communication

If someone's self-talk or story is that another person doesn't like them, then that story will impact their body language. They might subconsciously put their shoulders down, not make eye contact, speak in a defensive tone and generally act in a way that supports their story. The other person can and will subconsciously pick up on the defensive tone and body language, and they'll respond to it by not liking what they see, hear and get from that experience.

You've probably heard the saying, *If you're not feeling confident, act as if you are!* When we "act" a certain way, we take on the body language and communication of someone who is confident, and this is what we communicate.

Later in this book we have offered you a bonus: the confidence stance. It's a single combined body language gesture which communicates complete and total confidence. It's awesome in its powerful simplicity, and mightily effective.

7% of communication is at a conscious mind level

Dr. Birdwhistell, in *Kinesics and Context*, discovered that **only 7% of what we communicate is through the actual words we say**.

However, words are important, and in our highly linguistic world, we need to use them carefully, appropriately and confidently. If you want to build rapport with someone through words, there are three key areas you can focus on.

1. Key Words

We all have favourite words that we use. People might use words like *cool, awesome, fantastic* to describe the same event. When we use those words in our communication with them, it sets up a subconscious connection. On a physiological level, it creates a neurological match in the brain, and they experience that you have understood them and their message.

2. Common Experiences

When you meet someone new at a party or function, often the first question you ask to generate conversation is, *'How do you know the host?'* We do this to identify a common connection, so we can instantly have something to talk about. Confident communicators ask lots of questions. They are interested in creating and maintaining a connection with others through finding common ground.

Carol recently experienced the power of this when she met with Peter, a potential client. She noticed that he had an athletic build similar to those of swimmers and lifesavers. She asked him what sport he had played in the past, and he replied that he was a swimmer, and also a surf lifesaver.

Once Carol informed him of her family history and success in both those sports, the meeting became more and more comfortable. Why? Because they now had a common experience to share with each other, something to talk about. It set up a level of trust that would normally take a longer time to achieve.

3. Communication Preferences

We communicate using a distinct combination of communication styles, and the words we use reflect this. Despite the billions of people in the world, there are four communication preferences: Visual, Auditory, Kinesthetic and Data-digital. You will see, hear, get and learn about these preferences later in this book.

But for now, have you ever met someone and just 'clicked'? You felt like old friends and chatted comfortably. Maybe that chat included attempting to figure out from where you know each other, because you are positive you're met. This experience could be because you shared an instant rapport with them; perhaps they shared your communication preference. This means they used words, images and gestures that you could specifically relate to. In essence, they "spoke your language", and, since you spoke theirs, communication flowed easily and effectively.

The reverse can also occur. When you've encountered someone with a different communication preference, you may have found it difficult to talk to him or her. Did they bore you with details? Was their speech too fast? Too slow? Or did they simply not stop for breath? Whatever your communication gripe, the real issue is that they weren't speaking your language.

And your preference isn't limited to the spoken word; it shows through in your writing too. Have you ever felt miffed that someone replied to your long and friendly email with a seemingly terse three lines? That isn't an indication of how they feel about you; it is though, an indication that their communication preference is different.

When you can recognise someone's communication style, you can talk to him or her in their language. And you'll also be able to interpret what they are really saying. You can leave behind misunderstandings and enjoy confident communication. Read on for the how-to steps to confident communication.

chapter 5   the 4 communication preferences
– what they are and why you need to know them

what are the four communication preferences?

The four main ways of communicating are through **visual, auditory, kinesthetic** and **data-digital** preferences. There are some people in this world who mainly experience the world by what they **see (visual)**. Some mainly experience the world through what they **hear (auditory)**. For some it's about how they **feel** and the vibes they get about things **(kinesthetic)**. And for some they mainly experience the world through **facts, figures and data (data digital)**.

We are a mixture of all these and, unless we have a physical impairment, we can all hear, see, feel and think. However, we tend to prefer one or two of these over the others.

there used to be a belief that people were born confident

If you weren't one of those people, there was nothing you could do about it. In 1935, Dale Carnegie published his bestseller, *How to Win Friends and Influence People*. In it, he outlined a step by step process on how to become a better communicator. Since then we have seen major leaps in the development of human consciousness.

We are much more aware of our emotions, our self-esteem and our higher functioning needs. We are much more aware of our power and our ability to create our life the way we want it to be.

We can all communicate confidently. The more we learn about the mind, and the more discoveries quantum physicists make about "reality", the more we can know about ourselves. No longer is easy and successful communication limited to those "gifted few" who seemed to communicate confidently from the moment they learned to talk.

Being able to communicate clearly and confidently allows you to impress people, draw more opportunities into your life, help people more and generally make your life easier and simpler.

why do I need to know all four preferences?

If you want to be a confident communicator, you need to understand how you communicate and you need to understand how others communicate.

how come?

Because some people communicate differently to you.
Because you communicate differently to some people.
Because people need you to communicate in *their* language.
Because if you don't understand how someone communicates you will never be able to communicate effectively with them. Because when you understand their preference, you understand their behaviour, their thinking and their communication needs.

Then you can communicate with them in a way they need, in a way they process, in a way they see and hear and understand.

Before you read on, remember what we have already said about your own preferences: *"We have a mixture of all of these preferences and, unless we have a physical impairment, we can all hear, see, feel and think. However, we tend to have a preference for one or two of these over the others".*

our communication preference is exaggerated by our stress

In times of stress, we tend to "go into" our communication preference. Our preferences of behaviour – those things we are more comfortable with – come to the fore and we may find ourselves behaving in automatic and subconscious ways. Some communicators become loud and yell, others withdraw.

"Going into" our communication preference can mean we may delete certain pieces of information from our reality, and only subconsciously allow through our filter other types of information, such as what we can see or what we can hear. The rest of it we may not process—even though it is occurring around us.

how knowing all four communication preferences helped us

When we are teaching, training, and presenting, we know we have all four preferences in the room, so we cater for all of them. We provide notebooks and coloured pens, and use PowerPoint or Prezi with videos and pictures, to help our visual communicators see the information. We do hands-on activities to engage our kinesthetic learners. We also ensure the room feels comfortable to be in, so they can retain more information. We speak and play music to engage our auditory communicators with sound. For our data-digital communicators, we provide plenty of facts, figures and statistics, as well as references to more information they may choose to research.

Most importantly, we speak their language. We use key words, buzz words and the language of the four communication references. We will show you how to do this in a later chapter.

how knowing all four communication preferences helped others

We have taught this information to teachers who, at first dismissed it as being something they already knew. (In the 1980's, visual, auditory and kinesthetic learning styles were promoted within the Australian school system.) Yet, whilst they were familiar with differences in the learning styles of their students, and how to tailor their activities to meet their needs, most of them had never been shown the body language and spoken language of the four communicators.

When they learn and apply this, **they report meeting the needs of their students at a whole new level.** They also tell us that they could connect with students they had struggled with in the past, and this rapport was valuable in achieving key outcomes in their students learning.

how knowing all four communication preferences helps you

As you read through the following chapters, you may recognise parts of yourself or people you know in many of the different preferences. This is completely normal. It is also completely normal to recognise yourself in only one of the preferences.

Some people have what we call a "high predominant preference", so they may read this information and respond by saying, "The traits of the visual communicator look exactly like me." or "The auditory communicator absolutely sounds like me." Let's explore in more detail the four communication preferences.

chapter 6   visual communicators –
how others *see* what you communicate

We see the world as "we" are, not as "it" is; because it is the "I" behind the "eye" that does the seeing.
Anais Nin (1903-1977) French-American Poet

how a visual communicator behaves

Visual communicators pay most attention to what they are **seeing**. They often **think fast**, **move fast** and **talk fast**. The reason they move and talk so quickly is because **they are literally telling you what they are seeing**–both outside themselves and internally as they see it. They may **bounce from one thing to another**, with noted **enthusiasm**.

They often **point** to the things they are looking at. Their words will show their visual preference. They use words like *"see"*, *"show"*, *"vision" and "picture"*. They'll use phrases such as *"Show me", "I see what you mean"* and *"Picture this."*

Visual communicators are **"big picture"** in the way they view the world. They can become overwhelmed or irritated by the "small picture" aka the details. **To them, details are boring, overwhelming and draining**. Having to tolerate someone giving them reams of detail feels torturous. If someone's speech goes on and on and on, the words a visual communicator is receiving fuse into their head, until **all they hear is *'blah...blah...blah'*.**

It's akin to the experience we have when we hear a foreign language. At first, we make an effort to hold onto words, to process what they mean. After discovering we cannot make sense of what we are hearing, it's easier to allow the words to wash over us. Visual communicators can listen and listen well; they simply need to be spoken to in *their* language.

how a visual communicator behaves under stress

They want you to *see* that there is something wrong. This often manifests as a demonstrative showy performance and people may misjudge them as a "drama queen" or a "show off".

When stressed, their vision narrows and their usual ability to consider many things is reduced. To manage this and regain control, they may use a command style voice, which can offend others. This behaviour can be interpreted as bossy, when in fact they simply want to get things done.

One of our clients gave us a perfect and funny analogy of the visual communicator:

"A visual communicator is like a seagull. They fly in, squawk a lot, flap around, steal your chips and then leave…usually leaving those in the room in shock wondering what just occurred."

what is important to a visual communicator?

Appearances are very important as they care about how they look. They care about how their partner looks, They care about how their children look. They care about how their employees and colleagues look. They also care greatly about how the environment around them looks. Examples of this are wearing designer clothes, driving a luxury car, living in a nice house in the "right" suburb.

Because of this, people often make a judgement about them that they are shallow, and this is untrue and unfair. It's important to them that things look organised, clean, and pleasing-to-the-eye. It gives them energy when their working and living space is uncluttered, clean and clear. It drains them, when their visual environment is messy, dirty, disorganised or they see it as ugly.

The worst insult you could ever give a visual communicator is to tell them they or their environment e.g home, office, looks "bad" in some way. In fact, you may not even need to say the words. They are sensitive to the looks other people give them, so even looking them up and down with displeasure, or glancing around their environment with judgement could be devastating for them.

how do you know you are living or working with a visual communicator?

It's possible that the house or office looks tidy, yet the cupboards are messy. Why? You can't see what's behind the cupboard doors, of course. The mess is hidden; the illusion of calm and harmony remains. They may begin their day by sorting, cleaning or organising. They simply cannot work or relax if their environment is cluttered.

Our friend Peter told us about his partner who always runs around the house tidying before someone comes over. The problem is that later he can never find his things. When questioned, his partner replies, *'Where did you leave it in the first place? And what was it doing there?'* For a visual communicator, everything has a place and visual clutter can become overwhelming.

When a visual communicator communicates "big picture" sometimes this can come across as vague. They are often criticised for being vague or "flighty". They can lose respect in the workplace if they stay too "big picture" because they don't see the detail is necessary. They are **visionary** and can often plan many years ahead. When this skill is utilised in business, they make excellent future planners.

They are "high energy" people and they achieve a great deal very quickly. They can swoop into a home or an organisation, like a ballistic missile, offering solutions, making change and tossing out the dead wood. For someone not ready for change it can be devastating; however, for an organisation or environment wanting to step up to the next level, the results can be transformational.

how to communicate with a visual communicator
- ✓ Speak their language e.g *Let me **show** you what I mean. Here's an **image** to demonstrate my idea. **Picture** this.*
- ✓ Speak quickly and audibly (match your volume to theirs) and get to the point. Quickly!
- ✓ Show them something tangible e.g *Here's the cover for your new book. I printed it out for you so you can see what it looks like.*
- ✓ In written form, keep your information or request short, clear and direct. Excessive detail overwhelms them.

- ✓ If you have to give them detail, keep it brief, hand them a piece of paper with the key points, then sum up and take them back up to the bigger picture e.g *'So, your day looks like this. You've a meeting at ten to discuss the conference. Ming will need the numbers as well as your speaking topics. At twelve you've got the pitch with Lawton's and then a lunch at Cleo's. Lawtons need the final figures by COB tomorrow. At four you need to pick Bella up from the airport so you'll need to leave by three. So, summing up, conference meeting at ten with Ming, Lawtons at twelve plus lunch, final figures to Lawtons tomorrow and leave here at three for airport. Looks like a busy but fun day!'*
- ✓ When giving directions, draw them a map, give them landmarks, and even the map reference so they can see for themselves

If you *tell* them, they don't hear or remember it.
If you *go on and on and on* they switch off.
If you give them *detail*, they don't process it anyway...

...so, you may as well save yourself and them the time and effort, and communicate in a way they need.

how it helped us to see a visual communicator

When Carol, whose preference is visual, learned this information, it altered the way she receives directions. She realised that she becomes overwhelmed if someone gives her verbal directions. She struggles to take them in, hearing instead a stream of meaningless sounds. This may be accompanied by a string of meaningless images. It was exhausting and draining and a time-waster. She saw how many times she would listen to someone offer directions—nodding politely and smiling, because that's what most of us are trained to do, right? Externally, it appeared she was taking in the information. Internally, she felt sick, frustrated and overwhelmed.

Now, when she receives directions, she prefers to be given the map details, so she can **look** it up. If someone is giving her directions to an area she is familiar with, she prefers a **landmark** such as *'It's next to the grey building on the corner'* rather than a detail, *'Take the Northern Road heading west, then drive through 3 roundabouts, it's about 400 metres, then turn right at Church Street, but stay in the right lane because…'*

It was a liberating moment for her to clearly communicate her preference to someone, *'Thanks. All I need is the map address and a landmark'.* It is faster, more effective, confident communication and she appreciates knowing it.

how seeing this helps us

In understanding her visual preference, the biggest lesson Carol has learned is to be aware when she is feeling anxious or stressed, and to take a moment to ground herself before approaching others. This is so she does not overwhelm them with her fast, visual communication – which could place her out of rapport with them.

For Kathryn, whose main communication preference is *not* visual, it helps her remember to give the "big picture" – especially when working alongside someone with a high visual preference like Carol.

how knowing this helped others see a visual communicator

Jan, a client of ours, was having trouble dealing with her manager. She found her intimidating, especially in busier times. During weekly team meetings, Jan would helpfully provide an abundance of data to back up the great work she'd been doing. Her manager would abruptly dismiss her work, barely glancing at the data.

Jan recognised her manager is a visual communicator. She then understood that she didn't like going into the amount of detail which Jan had been providing. Now, she only offers an overview and a summary, which her manager glances at, while Jan and her colleagues discuss the data. She also includes several colourful graphs to appeal to her boss's visual communicating preference.

how it helps you to see a visual communicator

Many kinesthetic communicators we know would, in the past, often feel bombarded and intimidated by a visual communicator under stress.

Now, they can reframe that the person is simply having a stress reaction, and needs to be seen. They respond accordingly, by asking a simple question, offering support.

I see you are upset. Do you need to talk?
What do you need so things look clearer now?
Look at me and show me what we can do to get clear of this.

how visual communicators learn and remember

Visual communicators learn by seeing. They respond to demonstrations, PowerPoint presentations, and writing on the whiteboard, and they remember by writing the information down. For many visual communicators, it helps them to use coloured pens and draw diagrams.

When we share this information with corporate groups, we often hear a sigh of relief from those participants who need to take notes during meetings as a way to process data. In the past, this may have been misjudged by colleagues who thought they were not paying attention to the agenda or to the speaker, when in fact they were doing exactly that.

In a learning environment, a visual communicator enjoys seeing pictures and images. They remember this much more than the written word. In high school, they were the student who preferred to watch the movie rather than read the novel.

They also preferred the cliff notes or summary notes. Why? Because they were clear, succinct and gave them the highlights.

Highlights=Big Picture

visual communicators in their natural habitat

Typical jobs or hobbies of the visual communicator include:
- Designer
- Artist (painter, sculptor, animator, jeweller)
- Cinematographer
- Photographer

- Hairdresser
- Fashion designer and dresser
- Make-up artist
- Architect
- Media presenter
- Air Steward (because appearance is important)
- Entertainer (because they like to be seen)

Approximately 40% of the population have a visual preference, and the majority of these are female.

Visual Communicators like to be seen!

chapter 7   auditory communicators –
how others *hear* what you communicate

> ***The most important thing in communication is to hear what isn't being said.***
> Peter Drucker (1909 - 2005) American Management Writer

how an auditory communicator behaves

Auditory communicators pay most attention to what they **hear**. Their voice is **modulated** and **even**, and often sounds rather **melodious**. **They care about how they sound** and **they care about how other people sound to them**. They are **excellent listeners**, and are often the person people go to, to share problems.

When listening intently, they **tilt their head** and may even **cross their arms**. This is ***not*** **a defensive gesture;** they are actually listening, and this gesture helps them hear you better. However sometimes it can be interpreted as "closed" or "shut down". If you think you are *not* a good listener, and you want to improve your listening skills, this body language gesture is an excellent one to model.

An auditory communicator's words will show their auditory preference. They use words like **"hear", "listen", "sound"** and 'resonate'. They'll use phrases such as *"Are you **listening**?", "I'm all **ears**"* and *"I **hear** you."*

If they are upset, they will **tell you** or **complain**. They will do this **first in spoken form,** then **move to a written format** if they are not being heard. This is done to better communicate. They stop complaining when they are listened to, but people can stop listening to them because they are complaining. **They want you to hear that there is something wrong.** In a team environment, they can be misjudged as a "whinger", when all they are doing is expressing what is going on for them verbally. People often make a judgement about auditory communicators that they are "negative" or "complaining", when they are needing to be heard.

how an auditory communicator behaves under stress

If stressed, they become **sensitive to loud noises.** They may even place their hands over their ears to dampen down noise levels. They will become distracted by music, and it will impair their ability to work. If they are unable to control the sound within an environment such as at work, or on a plane, they'll use earphones to block out the noise.

They also become ***extremely* sensitive to tone of voice,** and their usual **ability to listen is reduced**. They are often labelled **"oversensitive"**. Others may feel the need to watch what they say around an auditory communicator, as they fear it may be misinterpreted. This is a valid and perceptive insight, as it is common for an auditory communicator to react to or judge the words which are said. This is because they measure words carefully and hold them with such value. Sometimes, it can feel like we are stepping through a minefield of words with an auditory communicator, never knowing which one will trigger a negative reaction. This is because words are important to them, much more important than images, feelings or information. For them, words are loaded with emotion.

When an auditory communicator perceives they are not being heard, and they are stressed, their communication becomes diminished. If they have expressed themselves with no good result, they may withdraw and give you **"the silent treatment"**. This is when they refuse to speak to you or acknowledge your presence, even if you are in their immediate vicinity. They will not respond to messages or email. They need space to process what has been said. Time will bring them out of their hibernation, as well as words of apology (if valid) or explanation, and **an assurance that you want to hear what they have to say**, will always be appreciated.

Do you remember the schoolyard chant, '*Sticks and stones will break your bones, but names will never hurt you!*' For someone with an auditory preference, this chant does *not* ring true. **It can be just as damaging to them hearing cruel words, as it can be to have someone physically hurt them.** They will often remember for years and years, things which were said to them in offence. And the worst insult you could ever give them would be to tell them they're a "bad" listener!

They also remember and are affected negatively by voices they don't like. This might include an accent, a strangulated tone or excessive volume. They react to "loud talkers", often finding visual communicators too loud and boisterous for their liking. They also dislike low volume, and it creates stress if they cannot hear a television, film or conversation. Although they love music, they tend to avoid venues such as pubs, clubs or restaurants with live music, as the noise level may create stress, interfering with their favourite past-time: conversation.

what is important to an auditory communicator?

We know that appearances are important to a visual communicator. So, what is important to an auditory communicator? They care greatly about what their environment **sounds** like. Examples of this are their choice of music, the sound of running water and peace and quiet. We know someone who installed an indoor waterfall, simply so he could hear the sound of rushing water every day.

An auditory communicator often wear headphones or earbuds as this enables them to control what they are hearing around them. In an open work environment, they may ask or demand peace and quiet, and may even remove themselves at times to get this. If things become too difficult, they may request to work from home, or move on to a job which better supports their auditory sensitivity.

how do you know you are living or working with an auditory communicator?

Their common phrase, if frustrated is, *'You are not listening to me!'* and they can become agitated when there is too much noise in their home. For example, when the television is up too loud, especially when the adverts come on, they can find it irritating. They detest those extremely loud advertisements, which push the volume to harsh levels.

They can become highly offended if called names, particularly offensive ones. If you are living with an auditory communicator, or in close relationship, and you are upset, it pays to stop a beat before you say something which may offend. They will always remember it...and you may always regret it!

When Kathryn's friend Jack visits her home, even if he's just popped in for a five-minute visit, he will ask her to turn the television or music down or off. He even puts his own playlist on if he's staying for longer. Because Kathryn knows about auditory communicators, instead of going into judgement or offense, she can accept her friend and his needs. She's learned that the fact he even asks, shows that he perceives her home as a comfortable space to hang out.

An auditory communicator will choose to live in auditorily calm and serene spaces. They may prefer the country to a noisy city; or they may choose an apartment based on the high-end, soundproofed double glazing. Anything to keep the harsh noise out!

how to communicate with an auditory communicator

- ✓ Speak their language e.g *Let me **tell** you what I mean. Here's some **words** and **sounds** to demonstrate my idea. **Listen** to this.* This will place you in rapport with them.
- ✓ Be aware of the words you use and their possible impact.
- ✓ When giving directions or instructions, you can tell them. They will recall most of what you've said.
- ✓ Be aware of your voice volume and tone. Keep it even, modulated and pleasant. Listen to their voice and use that type of voice back to them.

- ✓ Avoid speaking to them if you are angry or frustrated, even if it is at someone else. They may not be able to get past your "tone of voice" to hear what you are saying.

how it helped us to hear an auditory communicator

When Carol presents and facilitates, she has learned to monitor her voice. She is aware that, in the past, as a visual communicator, her voice tone would become "bossy" if time schedules were tight. She knows that she loses rapport with the auditory communicators if her voice tone is not calm, modulated and pleasant sounding.

Now, if she knows they are on a tight timeframe, she may even warn the auditory communicators in the room in advance, that she might be under time-pressure and this will change her tone. They then know she is not angry or being rude, simply attempting to teach them as much as she can within the time frame.

how it helped others to hear an auditory communicator

Susan had a revelation at one of our seminars. She realised her daughter was an auditory communicator. Commonly, her daughter came home from school, crying, as other children had called her names. Susan would console her, but say, 'Don't worry about it. It's only a name. It doesn't matter.' Realising that, for her daughter, the name calling was devastating, and why, was a profound parenting moment for Susan. Now she acknowledges her daughter's pain and has a way to support her out of her upset.

how it helps you to hear an auditory communicator

Sam, a tennis coach, realised that one of her squad members is an auditory communicator. She knows to be aware of her tone of voice with Courtney to keep it modulated and to only communicate encouragement. She knows that the more stressed Courtney is, the more sensitive she is to Sam's tone of voice.

Sam is also aware that, post-game, Courtney needs to hear a positive debrief, or she may even prefer to do it later. If you are managing an athlete who has an auditory preference, it may be best to talk to them beforehand, and ask them what they need in terms of feedback. This is so your well-intentioned advice is received and heard. More about this later when we talk about feedback filters in metaprograms.

how auditory communicators learn and remember

Auditory communicators learn by listening. They remember most of what they've heard word for word, and they don't need to take notes. They may have got into trouble at school because they didn't take notes and the teacher judged they were disengaged and not paying attention.

Often these same learners, when asked, could repeat back word for word what the teacher just said. As teachers, we observed this phenomenon many times. It's fascinating to see and listen to.

They learn through words: play on words, puns, word humour. They often report not remembering to learn how to read and write, simply finding they could.

They require a learning environment where the sound is balanced and even. If there is outside noise, excessive noise, unwanted noise or even noise of too poor a volume, their learning will be negatively impacted.

One of our clients sent her son to us because he suddenly developed "learning difficulties" at the start of a new school year. When we asked Ben what was going on for him at school, he replied, *'I can't stand my new teacher's voice.'* He had literally shut down his listening and therefore his learning capabilities, simply because he didn't like her tone.

We asked Ben whose voice he enjoyed listening to, and suggested he replace her voice with that one. In Ben's mind, his teacher now sounds like Bart Simpson! And unlike Bart, Ben's grades have gone back up.

auditory communicators in their natural habitat

Typical jobs or hobbies of the auditory communicator include:
- Sound engineer
- Musician
- Singer
- Counsellor
- Psychologist
- Psycho-therapist
- Sound healer
- Songwriter

- Composer
- Phone-based customer service operator
- Linguist
- Judge
- Audiologist
- Voice coach
- Translator

Approximately 20% of the population have an auditory preference.

When listening, an auditory communicator's head is often tilted to one side.

chapter 8   kinesthetic communicators – how others *experience* what you communicate

I pay no attention whatever to anybody's praise or blame. I simply follow my own feelings.
Wolfgang Amadeus Mozart (1756 - 1791) Austrian Composer

how a kinesthetic communicator behaves

Kinesthetic communicators pay most attention to what they are **feeling**. They often **move and talk slowly**. The reason they move and talk slowly is because they need to process everything through their feelings. It takes longer to do this than to simply process a thought, word or image.

Their language will show their kinesthetic preference. They use words like **"feel", "touch", "vibes"** and "grasp". They'll use phrases such as *'I get it', 'He's a cold person'* and *'Hang in there!'*

Kinesthetic communicators tend to stand in close proximity to others and like to be hands-on. If you are demonstrating something, they want to touch it, handle it, use it immediately. They gather data through touch. They often dislike galleries, exhibitions and museums—not because they find it boring or not of interest, but because they want to touch everything—and they are not allowed to!

Kathryn had an hilarious conversation with a group of her students about this. Every single one of her students who identified as a kinesthetic communicator, had been "busted" in an art gallery or museum for touching the displays. Alternately, a kinesthetic communicator will enjoy visiting places where they can "touch the merchandise": markets, hands-on aquariums, petting zoos, fabric stores and of course, anywhere in nature.

Kinesthetic communicators are welcoming and warm. They are particularly hospitable if you visit their home. We have a friend who is a kinesthetic communicator and we love taking new friends to her home. She greets them at the door with a big hug, feeds and nurtures them, takes time to get to know them, and says things like, *'Make yourself at home.'* Our friends leave feeling fantastic and incredibly loved–this is the charisma of a kinesthetic communicator in full flight!

how a kinesthetic communicator behaves under stress

If stressed, they can become overwhelmed with emotion and may even take days off work, for example they will take "stress leave", so they can process and isolate what is going on for them. It's very important for a kinesthetic communicator to remember there is a huge reality occurring around them. There are many things happening around them, which have nothing to do with them, and are none of their business. Some of the things they may have become caught up in, are other people's problems—it doesn't help others if a kinesthetic goes into someone else's drama. They benefit when they learn to step back and allow other people to solve their own problems and live their own lives.

It is vital for the kinesthetic communicator to discern what is their stuff and what is not, so they can put their precious energy into living their life to the best of their ability.

If they are upset, they will retreat. The reason they do this is because they're naturally sensitive to their environment. They can become overwhelmed with other people's emotions. They literally feel what other people are feeling and can take other's emotions on as their own. So not only do they have their own emotions to deal with, they may spend time dealing with other people's emotions as well. The biggest learning for them is to disconnect from other people's stuff.

If they can't physically retreat, for example being able to hide in the toilet or close the door to their office, they will retreat within, so they may become very quiet or non-responsive. If you ask a kinesthetic communicator who is upset, *'Are you OK?'* you will usually get one of two extremes; either a terse, *'Yep I'm fine'* with body language that says *Leave me alone*, or an emotional outburst about everything they are feeling. They will only do this if they know you well and trust you, or if they have been carrying so much they can't hold it in anymore.

what is important to a kinesthetic communicator?

We know that appearances are important to a visual communicator. Being heard, is important to an auditory communicator. So, what's important to a kinesthetic communicator? As we've mentioned, feelings and vibes are important to the kinesthetic communicator, and if they are in an environment of conflict or emotional turmoil, they will pick up on it straight away. When they walk into a place that is serene and peaceful, they'll often remark, *'The energy feels nice in here. I've got a good vibe about this place.'*

Their feelings and how they feel is important to them above all else. If they feel uncomfortable, they will close down and shut people out. If they feel comfortable, they blossom like a flower.

Kinesthetic communicators relate to the world through their body and how it feels. They get "good vibes" and "bad vibes" about things and they are rarely wrong. They feel what they are feeling. They feel what other people are feeling. They feel the mood in their environment. They feel the weather. They feel the trees and plants and flowers. They feel animals, and especially animals in pain. They feel, feel, feel.

At times, they can become overwhelmed with their feelings. We've known many a kinesthetic communicator to take a "sick day" if office tensions are high. And we've observed many children in our care tell us they 'feel sick in the tummy', when they are responding to an emotional event. When a kinesthetic sees advertisements for starving children or the homeless or impoverished, or hear of a threatened species, or violence or war, they feel overwhelmed. They feel tremendous empathy, but may also feel incapable of making any impact, which can make them feel guilty. They may avoid keeping up-to-date with world events, as they find the news "too negative" and the tragedy overwhelming. They need time out to process what they are feeling.

A kinesthetic communicator wants to be physical in their expression. Why? Because this is how they best experience the world. This is generally fine at home, but in the workplace, they can find the concept of "professional distance" challenging. They will often pat you on the shoulder or, link an arm through yours. If they feel they have good rapport with you, they may kiss you on the cheek or hug you which may be misunderstood or inappropriate in the workplace.

how do you know you are living or working with a kinesthetic communicator?

It's possible that their home will be furnished with comfy sofas, cosy furnishings and candles—anything that adds to the experience of "good vibes". Just as an auditory communicator may have music playing, and a visual will have an aesthetically visually pleasing environment, the kinesthetic communicator's home will feel comfortable and you will be welcomed.

They appreciate living on land or in the country. If unable to do this full time, they may have a holiday home in the country or by the sea; somewhere where they feel connected to nature. Their homes often have an indoor-outdoor component, such as a large balcony or a deck which moves out into a garden for entertaining. At the very least, they would prefer to see nature such as trees, greenery, water, when they look outside their home or office window.

Imagine this: a visual and a kinesthetic go shopping. They arrive at the shopping centre and the visual gets out quickly, walks down the main mall and past the shops, whilst quickly looking in each window, sees a shop she likes, goes in, scans for the right outfit, finds a dress, holds it up to the mirror, quickly tries it on and if it looks good she buys it. Meanwhile the kinesthetic communicator is still getting out of the car! You can imagine that visual and kinesthetic communicators don't necessarily make good shopping buddies.

If the kinesthetic communicator made it to the same shop, they would need to touch the fabrics. In search of an outfit, they would be after something that feels comfortable. Once they've found it, they may grab two sizes to try on for the best fit. They would need to feel good before buying something. If they don't feel comfortable in the shopping environment, they won't buy.

In the workplace it's important they trust their instincts around decisions, even though they may be questioned and asked to logically validate the reasoning behind their decision. They often remark *'This decision just feels right'*, and even though they don't need data or visual feedback to make a decision, it's important for them to get that other people do need this, and to supply it when appropriate. If managing a kinesthetic communicator, you may find over time that you trust their instincts on the "right" or "wrong" deal, client, customer or opportunity.

how to communicate with a kinesthetic communicator

- ✓ Speak their language e.g *Let's get a **feeling** for this. How does this **sit** with you? Do you **get** it?*
- ✓ Acknowledge their feelings as valid and real
- ✓ Where appropriate, allow them to be "hands-on". During a demonstration allow them to touch an item it or get up close.
- ✓ Some kinesthetics may need regular work breaks to stretch or take a brisk walk.
- ✓ If there is tension in your environment, allow them time out to process how they're feeling
- ✓ Lower your speed and tone of voice to match theirs. When you ask a question, allow them time to process before answering.
- ✓ Be patient if they seem slow. You may need to slow yourself down to stay in rapport.

how it helped us to meet a kinesthetic communicator

When Carol learned about kinesthetic communicators, she could see clearly why shopping with her long-time - friend Margot was so interesting. When Carol goes shopping, it is fast and purposeful (with a little bit of browsing!). Carol can walk into a shop and quickly scan to see if there is something worth trying on. Meanwhile Margot likes to touch the fabrics, only considers natural fibres and definitely won't look at or wear high heels. They head into completely different shops, then meet each other for lunch at a place they do agree on.

how it helped others to meet a kinesthetic communicator

One of our seminar participants, Andy, is a swimming coach. The week before he attended our workshop on communication, he had shown one of his swimmers, Josh, a new stroke. He'd explained why it was better and how it could shave precious seconds off his time. He'd given him the biomechanics behind the stroke. Yet Josh couldn't get it.

Andy realised Josh is kinesthetic, so he decided to communicate in the way Josh needed. With permission, he took Josh's arm and moved it through the exact movement of the stroke. This was then locked into Josh's muscle memory and he could perfectly reproduce this stroke from that point forward.

how it helps you to meet a kinesthetic communicator

Being aware of a kinesthetic communicator's needs means you can slow yourself down to their pace, placing yourself in rapport. You can speak slower and move slower and allow them time to process their feelings around any information you are showing or telling them.

Kinesthetics are extremely grateful when someone makes the effort to connect with them; they are all about connecting. When you take the time to do this, you will have their loyalty and devotion, and of course a continued easy rapport.

how kinesthetic communicators learn and remember

Kinesthetic communicators **learn by doing**. They respond to **"hands-on" and physical activities** in which they activate their highly refined muscle memory to recall most of what they do. Once they have grasped it, once it is "in their body", they can usually reproduce it perfectly, even a week or a month later. Many athletes and dancers have this ability.

When teaching a kinesthetic communicator, rather than demonstrate first, **let them do it with you**, either by demonstrating or talking them through it step-by-step. If you tell or show them first, they literally do not process what you are saying, and you are wasting your time and theirs. They need to do the steps as they receive them to get what you are teaching them.

kinesthetic communicators in their natural habitat

Typical jobs or hobbies of the kinesthetic communicator include:
- Athlete
- Dancer
- Dance teacher
- Park Ranger
- Massage therapist
- Landscaper
- Gardner
- Farmer
- Grower
- Childcare worker
- Tradesperson
- Labourer

A kinesthetic communicator feels less overwhelmed and more connected in nature.

Approximately 30% of the population have a kinesthetic preference.

chapter 9 data-digital communicators –
how others *understand* what you communicate

The significant problems we face cannot be solved at the same level of thinking with which we created them.
Albert Einstein, (1879 - 1955) US (German-born) Physicist

how a data-digital communicator behaves

Data-digital communicators pay most attention to **data, facts and figures**. Their **voice** is often **monotone,** with little fluctuation in tone, and **their gestures are minimal**, because they easily disassociate themselves from their emotions, and their body.

Their words will communicate their data digital preference. They use words like **"think", "process", "understand"** and **"data".** They'll use phrases such as *'I know', 'I understand'* and *'Let me analyse the components of the data'.*

Data-digital communicators are **detailed in their thinking**. They can become irritated by people who do not provide details, and may get judged for being too "picky". Yet for the data digital communicator, these details are extremely important and are how they make sense of their world.

A perfect example of this is asking a colleague in the workplace for an overview of the quarterly budget. A data digital communicator thinks in detail, so might reply by providing you with every single detail of that budget, including information that may be irrelevant to you or your role. Alternately, as they see data as precious and valuable, some data-digital communicators may guard their facts carefully, only revealing them when they are convinced of your need to see and process them. Other communication preferences can become overwhelmed or even annoyed by this behaviour, and so it may stop them from asking relevant questions, and receiving vital information.

The value of the data digital communicator is that they never miss any detail, they are excellent in industries concerned with quality control and health and safety. We feel assured boarding a plane, knowing that a data digital communicator has completed an extensive safety check and the plane is in top working condition.

When their skills are utilised in business, they make excellent accountants, IT technicians, doctors, surveyors, engineers and solicitors. As they can keep emotion out of things, they can manage difficult tasks such as layoffs and reducing budgets without becoming emotionally affected. They can also stay focussed during times of crisis. Imagine the chaos that could erupt in an emergency room if the attending doctor became too emotionally involved to make appropriate decisions around someone's health. Surgeons are usually data-digital in their preference, not only because they must have an ability to recall important data and details, but also because they are emotionally detached from what is occurring which gives them the ability to remain "on task".

how a data-digital communicator behaves under stress

If a data-digital communicator is upset or stressed, they tend to become "detail and data oriented". This means they may come across as being hard or uncaring, when they are simply going into their preference to make sense of things. In stressful times in the workplace, they may bring more and more details to people's attention. This communication can confuse and offend others, in particular a kinesthetic communicator, who may judge them as "cold" and "unfeeling". In a situation requiring empathy, they may display little. This does not mean they are not perceiving it. It simply means they are under stress, and have reverted to their stress response to manage themselves.

what is important to a data-digital communicator?

We know that appearances are important to a visual communicator. Being heard is important to an auditorily-preferenced person and feelings are important to a kinesthetic communicator. So, what's important to a data-digital communicator? **Details are important to them.** Data, Facts, Figures. It is very important they can communicate details to you. It is vital when communicating with them that, as a confident communicator, you provide details to them. They will expect them, and they will require them to make decisions.

how do you know you are living or working with a data-digital communicator?

It's possible that everything is ordered and has its place. Furnishings are minimal and practical, and the environment is often sparse, bordering on clinical. It will have the best technical equipment which is there for practical purposes.

Of the four communication preferences, we have found data-digital communicators less likely to manage relationships effectively. Many might claim that they are "loners" or say they are "just not a people person". Yet there is a specific explanation for this anomaly: data.

Approximately 10% of the population have a data digital preference, and the majority of them are male.

If you put a random cross section of one hundred people into a room, forty will tend to a visual communication preference and most that group will be female. Kinesthetic communicators will comprise thirty percent. Twenty people will be auditory communicators. But only ten people in that room will relate to the data-digital way of communicating.

When a data-digital communicator engages in the world, statistically there are a lot less of their own kind to interact with. What this means for a data digital communicator is there are a lot less people who tend to hold the same communication characteristics. **This means they can be naturally out of rapport with a lot of people**; in particular, the visual communicator who is focussing on "big picture" and "vision", who becomes bored with their detail. They are often out of rapport with the kinesthetic communicator who talks the language of feelings, and may find them "cold" or "unfeeling" and their home or work environment "clinical". An auditorily preferred person may find the voice of a data digital communicator unstimulating, so they "switch off".

A data-digital communicator may move through life experiencing constant mis-matches with others. No wonder they become relieved or even excited when they find someone else with whom they can share details and swap data. **It's vital they acquire the skill of mirroring so they can place themselves in rapport with the people they are interacting with.** Naturally, their confidence in communication will increase.

We have two friends who go into their data-digital preferences when talking computers. If we are all out together and they start talking "computer talk", it is as if they are speaking another language. We can't understand what they are talking about. The more they communicate, the more data-digital they become, and they put themselves out of rapport with the group.

Understanding their preference, and because we know they understand their preference as well, we'll often "call them back" by gently teasing them about their "techie talk".

how to communicate with a data-digital communicator

- ✓ Speak their language e.g *'I **understand'*** and *'Let me get that **data** to you.'* *'Thanks for the **information***'.
- ✓ Speak at a **moderate, even pace** and keep your voice **monotone**
- ✓ Avoid excessive hand gesture or movement
- ✓ When interacting in a work situation, give them the information they require. They do not need an emotional story to accompany it.
- ✓ In written form, keep your information or request brief, and only give the information required.

how it helped us to understand a data-digital communicator

Our friend Michael, who has a data digital preference, is well known for providing us with detail. Asking him, 'How was your swim?' will unleash a detailed ten-minute explanation of each step of his swim including data, facts and figures. It can sound something like this: *'It took me twelve point three seconds to swim the third lap and I realised that if I adjusted my elliptical-pull-pattern five degrees then I would be able to move faster through the* water. So, I made the adjustment, and timed the next lap, and I swam it in twelve-point-one-seven seconds.'

You may have had this experience with someone in your life. These people can overwhelm others with details which for them are truly fascinating, and yet may not be as interesting for others. A visual communicator may hear 'blah...blah...blah...' Some communicators, can become bored listening to the detail, or find it "disconnected" or "too robotic".

For us, the value of knowing about confident communication lies in understanding Michael and his needs. Instead of writing him off as boring, we see, hear and get those details are important to him. And he's important to us, so we listen to them.

how it helped others to understand a data-digital communicator

Carol worked with a data-digital engineer called Benjamin. He spent his day managing tradespeople: carpenters, plumber and electricians. From his office, Benjamin would send his team daily emails with requests for information. His team would ignore him. They judged him as aloof and did not do as he asked. He had little rapport with them.

When Benjamin learned this information about confident communication, he changed the way he interacted with his team. Recognising most of them were kinesthetic, and that he was data-digital, he ceased his email communication. Instead he spent time with his team hands-on, communicating with them, checking in on their feelings, and mirroring their body language. Benjamin placed himself in rapport and, like magic, his team willingly and happily completed all the tasks he set them. Recognising how his data-digital communication style had placed him out of rapport, gave him the knowledge to communicate effectively with his team.

how it helps you to understand a data-digital communicator

It's possible that, of the four preferences, the data-digital communicator is the most judged. Visual communicators often see them as boring. Kinesthetics may perceive them as cold and disconnected. Auditory communicators may hear their voices and switch off.

Yet, just as each human being has value, so does each communication preference. If we judge or dismiss someone, we close ourselves off to possibility, we stop ourselves from potentially receiving something we may want or need. **We** miss out.

You may not choose to socialise with differing communicators, but you can choose to gain and stay in rapport with them, thus ensuring effective and confident communication in your lives and the lives of all those with whom you interact.

how data-digital communicators learn and remember

Data digital communicators learn by asking questions to make sense of the detail in front of them. They respond to any factual information such as statistics, references and latest research which they will debate with you enthusiastically.

At school, they may have found themselves in trouble for asking too many questions or questioning the teacher. This can follow them into the workplace where people may become threatened by their questions and feel as if their abilities are being questioned.

Data digital communicators are often quick to comprehend ideas and concepts. **Their most commonly used phrase is *'I know'*,** and even though others might get annoyed by this or think it arrogant, they really do know. They seem to receive information quick-as-a-flash and in whole chunks, so even when someone is half way through explaining a concept, the data digital has already processed the entire message. Their usual response is *'I know'* and it can be off-putting for the speaker, especially an auditory communicator who may feel not listened to.

Often, they don't know how they know things–they just know that they know. Sometimes they resent having to justify *how* they got to an answer; they just did. These were the kids in your maths class who just "knew" the answer without knowing "how". They may have been accused of cheating or been asked to show their working as they hadn't included any.

data-digital communicators in their natural habitat

Typical jobs or hobbies of the data-digital communicator include:
- Doctor
- Surgeon
- Mathematician
- Computer designer
- Computer technician
- Software developer
- Inventor
- Quality control
- Pilot
- Scientist
- Surveyor

This is a data-digital male sharing a concept he is passionate about. Note his bland facial expression, controlled stance and minimal hand gesture.

Approximately 10% of the population have a data- digital preference, and the majority of them are male

chapter 10 when the sh*t hits the fan – what can happen when these four communicators get together and what to do about it

how on earth do we communicate with anyone?

Given that we have a large reality occurring around us, that we are only consciously aware of a small amount of this "reality", and that, layered on top of this there are four quite different ways of perceiving the world, with four different "languages" spoken–even if they're all speaking English–it's an absolute wonder that any of us can get our message across at all.

Interesting dynamics come into play when the four different communication preferences begin interacting. Communicators can become frustrated, bored, offended or misunderstood. They can feel disabled, disheartened and disillusioned.

The most important thing to remember is that none of us perceive reality as it actually occurs. We only experience our limited perception of reality, because no matter how open minded we may be, our brain still has limits around its own ability to process information. When we remember that everyone is right according to their own model of the world, it frees us up now to allow for a win-win in every situation.

You now see, hear, get and know some of the secrets confident communicators use. You learned how to observe and "mirror" body language so you can place yourself in "rapport". You know how easy this is to do now because your subconscious mind is already an expert at this.

You also learned how to "break rapport" when needed. Whether it's "visual", "auditory", "kinesthetic" or "data-digital", you know how to identify your own preferred "communication preference" in others, as well as spot specific communication preferences. You can now use their language when speaking with them.

You now see, hear, get and understand why people behave in specific ways when stressed, and you know what to do about this. You know how to manage people more easily to maintain happy and harmonious living spaces. As a six-year-old we know often says with immense enthusiasm... *'Good job!'*

Following are some key points to be aware of when considering the interactions between the different preferences. They are a general guide, however if you have ever experienced conflict with someone, this section may give you an insight into the reasons why.

visual communicators interacting with auditory communicators

When visual communicators go into stress they develop a command style voice aka *they sound bossy*. They give commands and orders in a bid to sort through their stress and see things more clearly. This can offend the auditory listener who may hear an offensive or rude tone even when it's not intended.

As visual communicators move quickly from one thing to another, often glancing around, even when engaged in conversation, an auditory communicator may perceive they are not being listened to. When a visual communicator is being listened to, they may see the "crossed arms" gesture of an auditory communicator as a defensive barrier, when in fact they are being heard. And seen.

visual communicators interacting with kinesthetic communicators

Visual communicators naturally move at a faster pace. They talk fast, move fast and even think fast. They can become impatient with the slower pace of a kinesthetic communicator.

They tend to get on well together if they can acknowledge mutual strengths. They then balance each other out: the kinesthetic communicator enjoys the high energy and vivaciousness of a visual, while the visual communicator can enjoy and benefit from the calm pace of those with a kinesthetic preference.

The behaviour of an extremely high visual who is constantly talking and moving can become overwhelming for a kinesthetic communicator, and they want space to feel calm again.

visual communicators interacting with data digital communicators

Visual communicators are "big picture" and want to get things done quickly...as in **right now**! A visual communicator will want to find the shortest way to achieve an outcome. Data-digital communicators are detailed and methodical, and will take all the time they need to follow a process to its conclusion. This combination creates an interesting dynamic when interacting.

Visual communicators can learn that sometimes details are important, and processes can be useful. Data-digital communicators can learn that sometimes there is a faster way than following a set process, and that flexibility is important in human interactions.

auditory communicators interacting with kinesthetic communicators

If an auditory communicator is under stress, they tend to complain aloud. This can be overwhelming for a kinesthetic preference as they naturally feel what the auditory communicator is feeling, and want to do something to fix it. The kinesthetic tendency is to ask, "How are you feeling?" which the auditory communicator may find annoying, particularly if they are still processing what's going on for them.

auditory communicators interacting with data-digital communicators

These two preferences tend to interact easily, however an auditory communicator may become offended or bored by the data-digital tone of voice, which can be monotone and unemotional. It makes it hard for them to listen to content if the delivery does not sound interesting. A data-digital may interrupt an auditory communicators message mid-way with a comment such as "I know!", causing the auditory communicator to perceive they are not being listened to.

However, remember the concept of blame vs responsibility? There are many situations we cannot control and, whilst it's easy to blame the messenger, their information may be something we need to hear. So, an auditory communicator may benefit from internally altering the voice they are listening to. Just as ten-year-old Ben changed his teacher's voice to sound like Bart Simpson, changing what they hear to a more preferable tone or accent can assist an auditory communicator in receiving the information.

A data-digital communicator may find that when they take the time to listen to the entire message, they stay in rapport with an auditory communicator. It's also possible that, sometimes, they may find they missed vital data as they cut the speaker off too soon.

data-digital communicators interacting with kinesthetic communicators

The data digital communicator's world is based on data. The kinesthetic communicator's world is based on feelings. One is tangible, perceptible and quantifiable. The other is nebulous, changeable and not able to be quantified in any scientific fashion.

The kinesthetic communicator may perceive the data-digital as dismissing their feelings–which are real to them, and they may judge a data-digital as "hard", "cold", "uncaring" and "unsupportive". The data digital communicator may perceive that the kinesthetic communicator is vague, over-emotional or airy-fairy. Both responses have their appropriate place in our world. The key to happy, confident interaction is to withhold judgement and remember we all perceive the world differently, ergo, someone may have an insight from which we can benefit.

chapter 11 which communication preference am i? – a quick quiz

© *Copyright Kathryn Gorman 2006*
Amended from Tad James, Advanced Neuro Dynamics, 2000

To answer, read all four options and circle your FIRST and INSTANT response:

1. When you enter a room you pay most attention to:
a) How it looks
b) The things you can hear e.g music
c) The feeling in the room e.g good vibes, cold room
d) Specific details and technology in the room

2. When you meet a new person, you form an impression based on:
a) Their appearance and how they look
b) Their voice and the things they say
c) The gut feeling you get from them
d) Their qualifications or position

3. When you make a decision, it is mainly based on whether it:
a) Looks right
b) Sounds right or
c) Feels right i.e "Gut feel"
d) Data and logic; it makes sense

4. When you buy new clothes or furniture, your main consideration is:
a) How they look and that they are the latest trend or fashion
b) How they sound e.g the sound of the sofa swooshing as you sink into it
c) That they feel comfortable and cosy
d) That they are a good investment and high quality, and include the latest technology

5. To cheer someone up, you would most probably:
a) Show something to distract them from what they're upset about
b) Say something helpful
c) Offer them a hug
d) Give them information

6. *To determine if someone is doing a good job, you prefer to:*
a) See them do the job, or see graphs, diagrams etc that they have produced
b) Hear them doing their work or telling you about what they did
c) Do the job with them or experience some aspect of their job
d) Have all the information, facts and figures on the work that's been done

7. *In a learning situation e.g conference, seminar, you prefer:*
a) Things you can see, such as PowerPoint, or information presented in pictures, diagrams and images
b) Mostly listening, such as a presenter talking
c) To learn by doing an activity or exercise
d) Information presented in facts, figures and statistics so you can make sense of it

8. When employing or hiring someone e.g at work, babysitter, builder, you would tend to:
a) Hire the person who looks the most suitable and trustworthy
b) Base your decision on the things they tell you
c) Hire the person you get the best "good vibes" about whom you feel the most comfortable with
d) Hire them based on their qualifications and the details they offer

9. Which best describes you? You find that you:
a) Have a strong response to colours and to the way life looks
b) Are very attuned to the sounds in my environment
c) Are very sensitive to other people and how they are feeling
d) Prefer to deal with facts and data than people

10. If being praised, you prefer:
a) Feedback that you (and others) can see e.g sales chart
b) To be told
c) A physical reward e.g a bonus, trophy, day off
d) Data or figures backing up the reason for the praise

add up your scores:
a = ____ (visual)
b = ____ (auditory)
c = ____ (kinesthetic)
d = ____ (data-digital)

rank your results (by circling):
1st preference: v   a   k   d-d

2nd preference: v   a   k   d-d

3rd preference: v   a   k   d-d

4th preference: v   a   k   d-d

please don't put me in a box

Our intent in sharing this information is so you can see, hear, get and know insights about yourself or someone else. This can make your life simpler and easier through utilising the skills and secrets of a confident communicator.

This quiz is *not* intended to be a way for you to "label" yourself, or others, (labelling=judgement) nor is it an excuse for inappropriate behaviour. However, as human beings we do require guidelines around specific behaviour. The gathering of common characteristics, can enable us to draw certain conclusions which assist us in more effective and confident communication.

We used to offer this quiz as part of our workshops. We found that certain personalities became so caught up in the "label" or the fear of being labelled, they couldn't move beyond it and they missed the point of the exercise, as well as missing a chunk of valuable information as the workshop moved on.

Any quiz or questionnaire can only ever give you a guide or general indication of your preferences in any situation. Doing this quiz will give you an indication of your preference for one of the four ways of communicating over the others. We can however access all four ways and may relate to aspects of each of these.

When doing this quiz, some people find they have one very clear preference. Others find they have even preferences spread amongst all four areas. **There is no right and no**

wrong. It's our combination of preferences and quirks that makes us unique and human. If you still want further clarification on this area, go to chapter 16, where you can identify your main way of communicating in a decision-making context.

We hold an intention that, at the end of our workshops, or at the end of you reading this book, if you have a new perspective, fresh angle or another insight around someone in your life, then we have achieved our goal. If reading this book has caused you to sigh with understanding, lovingly giggle a little at yourself or someone you know, or possibly see with new eyes, this makes *us* happy and confident communicators. And it makes *you* one as well.

These ways of communicating can serve you in understanding more about yourself and others. They can assist you in becoming a confident communicator. If doing this quiz or reading this book has allowed you to see, hear, get or know something that you didn't know before, and this helps you in your life, then that is worth it, isn't it?

primary and secondary preferences

Remember when we said how some people identify strongly with one communication preference and others will identify with more than one? Identifying with more than one way of communicating is called a "preference combination". There are some common preference combinations which are interesting and, for the sake of increasing confident communication skills, we wanted to mention these here.

Please note these labels can be interchanged, so if your preference combination is Kinesthetic-Visual then the information for Visual-Kinesthetic preference will be relevant.

visual – kinesthetic preference

Someone with a visual–kinesthetic preference tends to be popular. As their two preferences are the most common statistically, this combination finds themselves in rapport with approximately 80% of the population automatically, just by being themselves and talking their own language.

Therefore, they are often perceived as "good with people" and can be dynamic and visionary leaders and managers. They are high-energy people and very caring of others. They are often the life of the party and everybody's friend. When they also interact with and relate to the auditory and data-digital communicators, including them in their world, this is a confident combination.

kinesthetic – auditory preference

The combination of feelings and listening skills make this double preference caring childcare workers, music therapists and counsellors. They are also extremely sensitive, as they feel things deeply and are so affected by the things people say.

It is important for them to learn to manage this, so their "super sensitivity" doesn't become so extreme that it's difficult for them to live in the world and interact with others. They can do this by remembering that we all have our own perception of reality. Every perception or model of the world is valid. It helps them to believe or remember that generally people are just acting from their own perception, rather than consciously saying or doing things to be purposely offensive.

visual – data digital preference
This can be an interesting combination. The visual component likes to be "big picture" and get things done quickly, whilst the data-digital component likes to be detailed and methodical.

What this preference holds is an ability to plan "big picture", as well as the skill and patience to follow through each specific step needed to bring an idea to fruition. These skills are extremely useful in areas such as financial planning, law, economic forecasting, futures trading and upper management. You would also see them in industries that combine detail with visual intelligence, such as graphic design or fine art.

data-digital – kinesthetic preference
In our workshops and coaching, we see this preference mostly among males, and commonly among athletes. This preference has the awareness of feelings, vibes and their effect on others, as well as an ability to be detailed and detached when necessary.

They learn details through practical application, and possess the ability to store and recall specific details, reproducing them when necessary. They have an excellent body and environment awareness; very important in an athlete for example, yet can go to that detached place in their head. As an athlete, this enables them to push through the pain barrier.

It's important for this preference to allow their kinesthetic tendencies to balance out their data-digital preference, so they can be appropriately connected and caring. This helps them maintain rapport particularly in the workplace, as it allows them to relate to more people. As well as athletes, you may see this preference amongst coaches and personal trainers who work with elite athletes, where analysing micro body movement means the difference between winning and losing.

visual – auditory preference

This preference is typical amongst singers, performers, actors, talk show hosts, and those in the entertainment industry. The visual component means they care about their appearance and how they are seen, and this is a priority for them. They'll do what it takes to look good and maintain it e.g: high fashion, gruelling gym workouts and diets.

The auditory component means they have a beautiful melodious voice, which is pleasing on the ear, a vital skill in entertainment. They also possess a natural aptitude for listening, can "read between the lines", and most of the time they only need to hear things once to recall them; the latter is a useful skill when taking direction and recalling lines of a script.

data-digital – auditory preference

This combination of preferences is held by only a small percentage of the population. The auditory component means they value listening and being listened to, yet their data-digital component often uses technical jargon that others don't understand.

It could be a challenge for them to find others who will listen and truly understand what they are saying. It's important for them to hear that others are doing their best to listen and process what they say.

They usually make excellent students, as they grasp concepts quickly and can recall most of what is said to them. They usually do well in exams, as they have the ability to disconnect emotionally and see the task for what it is–an opportunity to recall and analyse data to prove how much they have learned. As words are important to them, they do well in a field which requires analysis of words such as interpreting, editing, publishing, technical writing and proof reading.

chapter 12   figure it out –
identifying communication preferences and why you might want to

By now, you've possibly figured out your own communication preference, as well as those of the key people in your life. Perhaps you've identified your partner as a visual communicator and now understand why you become angry when, during conversation, they look around the restaurant instead of at you. Now you know, don't you, that it is possible they are actually listening to you, while continuing to gather visual data to see the world more clearly.

Maybe you've correctly identified your manager as a data-digital communicator, and you've resolved to give them *only* the information they need from now on. Now you can get why they don't need to hear the story about how your car broke down on the motorway this morning making you late for work. Even if you really, *really* need to tell it.

And instead of becoming annoyed with your daughter's silent treatment, or secretly labelling her a "whiner" and a "whinger", now you see, get and understand that your child is an auditory communicator. She needs to be heard! And you can listen to her now, can't you? And you'll all live happily ever after...

Doesn't it look, sound and feel awesome to understand these behaviours now? Confident communicators do. And one of the key differences between an average communicator and an effective one is an effective communicator applies these skills and understanding *all the time.*

Does it take some effort to learn this? Yes. Will you need to invest some time in fine-tuning these skills? Yes. Is it worth it? Yes. Absolutely, yes. It changed our lives for the better, and it can change yours too. But only if being a confident communicator is important to you, of course.

The chart on the next page outlines the key components of each communication preferences at a glance. It's a useful tool to have nearby, as you are learning and practising how to communicate confidently with all four communication preferences now.

the four communication preferences at a glance

	body language	voice	words & phrases
visual	- Fast - Pointing gestures - Active hands - Breathe high in chest - Eyes up - Head up and straight	- Fast - Loud - High pitched - Nasal	'*I **see** what you mean.*' '***Look** at that!*' '***Show** me.*' '***Picture** this...*'
auditory	- Folds arms - Head tilts to side - Full range of breathing - Eyes side to side	- Modulated - Clear - Resonant - Balanced & even	'***Listen** to me.*' '*I **hear** you.*' '***Sounds** good.*' '*That **rings** a bell.*'
kinesthetic	- Slow - Upturned palms & arms bent - Breathe from abdomen - Eyes down - Head relaxed	- Slow - Soft - Low & deep - Long pauses	'***Feels** good.*' '*I **get** it!*' '*I don't **feel** like it...*' '*Get a **hold** of this.*'
data-digital	- Minimal movements - Stand upright with head up - Constricted breathing - Minimal eye-contact	- Monotone - Clipped - Even - Considered	'*Do you **understand**?*' '*I **think**...*' '*That **figures**.*' '*Let me **process** that.*'

chapter 13   how to speak another language – and why you might need to

why you need to speak another language

Each of the four communication preferences has a "language" which reflects the way they perceive the world. ***These are seen, heard, experienced and understood as four different languages.***

Have you ever had the experience of explaining something which you think is very clear and obvious, yet someone did not seem to hear you, or see you, or process what you have said. You may have repeated yourself several times, yet it was obvious your message wasn't received. The person you were communicating with may have been looking at you, yet their eyes glazed over and they didn't seem to "compute".

Perhaps there was nothing wrong with your clear and concise explanation. The problem may instead have arisen because you were talking a "different" language to them. Perhaps you were using kinesthetic words and they are primarily data-digital in their thinking. Or maybe you used auditory words, yet they are mainly visual in the way they perceive their world.

You might as well have been speaking *Klingon*.

This might sound simplistic, yet we have observed time and time again the effectiveness of using the "right" words for someone's communication preference, and seeing their face light up as they process our message. In our masterclass workshops we demonstrate the power of this.

the power of speaking the "right" language

In a recent workshop, Carol invited Kalinda to the stage. Kalinda presented as a high visual communicator. Carol proceeded to put two "proposals" to Kalinda, asking the group to observe for subtle changes on their face as she "spoke Kalinda's language".

The first proposal she presented, was purposely given in a "language" which is not Kalinda's communication preference: *data- digital*; the second was given in a language she is fluent in: *visual*, using words and phrases she commonly uses. It went something like this:

*'Kalinda, I have two proposals for you. Here's the first one. I'd like you to **process** some **information** for a job and I need you to **understand** and **explain** the **details** to **seventeen** of our managers. We think the **data** needs some **adjusting**. You will be required to gather **statistical data** and work **systematically** through each **process** until...'*

We heard giggles from the audience as they observed Kalinda considering Carol's proposal. By the time Carol was half way through the first sentence, Kalinda's eyes had glazed over. Although she was attempting to be polite, and listen, her face became dull and uninterested. She looked incredibly bored even though she was trying to maintain interest out of respect for Carol. She nodded slowly, then stopped, as the data continued to wash over her. She peered at Carol, then glanced around the room, squinting into the distance, as if to bring what she was hearing into focus.

Most of the group were quietly laughing at her very uninterested reaction. This language was, of course, very data-digital (*we bolded it for you to make it obvious*) and this language did *not* capture Kalinda's attention in a positive way. Carol then offered a second proposal:

*'Kalinda, I have a second proposal I want to **show** you. I'd like you to **look** at some **pictures** and **diagrams** and I need you to **clearly see** it and **show** the **vision** to some of our team. We **see** that it needs some changes. I'll need you to **envision** an ideal **picture** of where we are **heading** with this project. I'll need to **see clearly** your **vision** in **images**, so I'd appreciate **pictures**, **photos**, **sketches** ...'*

Carol smiled as the audience burst into laughter. Kalinda's face was alight with excitement. As soon as Carol began to speak, Kalinda commenced nodding enthusiastically and did not stop. Her face lit up and she couldn't stop herself from smiling, as the proposal mainly consisted of visual language which is Kalinda's preference. (*Again, we have bolded it for you.*) She gazed at Carol, stepping forward with one leg as if ready to get moving on the project!

Kalinda was totally and immediately interested in this second proposal, as it was the language of a visual communicator–her preference. When asked, which proposal looked more interesting to her, she laughed as if it were a no-brainer. *'The second one of course. I know it's the same job, yet the second one looks so much more interesting.'*

When asked what was the difference between the first proposal and the second, her reply was, *'The first one looked incredibly boring. The second one looked exciting, fun, more like something I'd enjoy doing.'* She then added, *'When can we start!'*

How many times a day do we speak a language to someone that they do not understand? How many times a day do we speak a language to someone that they do see, hear, get or process? This is not only useful in a business or sales context. **Whether we are selling an idea in a meeting, offering a new possibility, or even asking a child to tidy their room, we need to speak their language to them.**

Confident communicators consciously speak someone's language. All the time. Every day. To everyone. Every time they speak.

It's worth noting that Kalinda had no idea what the project was. It didn't matter. The secret was in how it was presented to her.

During our workshops, we show our participants how to watch for "sensory acuity". These are the physiological (body) changes evident on someone's face when they like or dislike something. These are subconscious reactions that cannot consciously be controlled. Blushing is an example of this.

A confident communicator is aware of these changes and observes them, so they know when they have communicated effectively. You can practise speaking other people's language as you interact day to day. You may even discover, as lots of our workshop participants have, that there is one language you find particularly, challenging and, in this case, it does require some practice.

When Kathryn first learned this, she discovered that she never used data-digital words. What this meant was there was a group of people whose language she never spoke, and she certainly found in her classroom that, no matter her efforts, there were always two or three students she felt she never reached or connected with. When she began using data-digital words in her teaching, the effects were amazing. Her student's faces lit up, and they approached her after class, wanting to share exciting information and discoveries.

If you've travelled to a foreign country, or immersed yourself in a culture where your mother-tongue is not spoken, you may find yourself gravitating to someone who speaks your language. Our friend Matt worked in China for three years, utilising the services of a translator during work hours. The translator was the only person he spoke English with, which meant the translator was the only person he had a conversation with in his mother-tongue during his day.

Whilst visiting a nearby town on his day off, Matt heard someone speaking English in the street. He tells us he literally vaulted through market stalls and over boxes of produce to introduce himself to this man. They ended up sharing a meal, in which Matt says he did not stop to draw breath, so happy was he to speak and speak and speak.

Seeing as we speak the language of our natural communication preference, it makes sense that we will attract people who "speak our language", because our words, voice and body language will naturally be the same. We will hear them "talk our language" and respond.

Remember the exercise of mirroring someone which we spoke of earlier? We automatically mirror people we like. So why not consciously do this with everyone? **This includes mirroring the words people use.** After all, if you went to Italy, it would make sense as an English speaker to approach people speaking in Italian, wouldn't it? It's the same with these four languages. **Talk someone's language and you will be assured of greater and more effective confident communication.**

Following is a list of common words used by the four communication preferences. As you are learning to identify each preference, it's useful to refer to this list. When we were learning it, we would keep the list nearby, especially when sending emails or speaking on the phone.

As the person is speaking, or as you read an email, **you can listen and watch for the "language" words they're using. Simply direct your subconscious mind to alert you to this.** Once you've identified someone's preference, you can use the same words in your responses to gain and maintain rapport.

As with any worthwhile skill, this takes a little practice, and it is so worth the effort when your communication is clearer, and you have instant rapport with the important people in your life.

Over the telephone, you can also **mirror the speed, volume, tone and pauses of the speaker**. If someone is speaking quickly, you will maintain rapport when you speak quickly to them. If their voice is low and slow, consciously make your voice lower and slower to stay in rapport with them for effective communication. If they speak loudly, match their volume.

This may seem weird, strange or feel uncomfortable at first, yet **it is almost like magic how doing this puts you in rapport with someone and assists you in communicating confidently.**

useful words & phrases to speak another language

visual	auditory	kinesthetic	data-digital
See	Hear	Feel	Digital
Look	Listen	Touch	Abstract
Peek	Sound	Grasp	Idea
Vision	Resonate	Concrete	Understand
Map	Silence	Scrape	Information
Appear	Blabbermouth	Hard	Process
Show	Tune	Soft	Learn
Visualise	Tune in	Vibes	Think
Picture	I'm all ears	Hot	Thought
Flashy	Rings a bell	Cold person	Know
Focussed	Are you listening?	Handle it	Data
Diagram		Boils down to	Facts
In light of	Word for word	Hang in there	Concept
Clear cut	Give you a bell	Throw out	Program
Dim view	It's unheard of	Hold on	System
Crystal Clear	Loud and clear	Sharp as a tack	Process this
Take a peek	Listen here	Slip through	That figures
Have a vision	Listen to me	All washed up	Adjust the figures
I see what you're saying	Tune out	Get a grip	
	It's very sound	In the groove	Define that
Look here	I heard you	Make contact	The data proves
Showing off	Loud and clear	He's a pain in the neck/butt	Conceptually viable
Picture this	Bend your ear		
How's that look?	Call on	Good feeling	I have an idea
	Call me	Catch you later	What do you think?
See you soon	I'm listening	Grasp at	
Show me	How does it sound?	Tap into	Systems think
I see	I hear you	I get it	I know

helpful tip: *Copy this list and place it near your workspace to refer to when you are on email or speaking on the telephone.*

chapter 14   chill out –
how to use communication to diffuse a tense situation

speaking people's language for conflict resolution

We are purposely keeping this chapter brief, as you have already learned the secrets which, when applied to any situation increase communication. When we examine the area of conflict resolution, the reality is simple: tense situations are only tense because someone see, hears, feels or thinks they are not being seen, heard, got/felt or understood. And conflict only escalates, because someone continues to mis-communicate – even if they are attempting to "help", "assist" or *'do the right thing'*.

how others used communication to diffuse a tense situation

Kathryn has a friend called Phil. Phil is a mild-mannered, gentle, auditory-kinesthetic. He's brilliant with people because he has innate communication skills. Several years ago, new neighbours moved in next door to Phil. They were loud, party dudes, whose favourite past-times were blaring heavy metal music, lifting weights and tinkering with their car in the driveway late at night, whilst they swore playful obscenities at each other as they fine-tuned their motors.

Phil's baby daughter's bedroom backed onto this driveway, and it was interrupting sleep patterns for the entire household.

During the day, at a decent hour, Phil tried speaking to these guys, explaining he had a baby in the house, and asking them to keep their noise down. He told us they were tough blokes. They were tall and muscly and huge, and he felt unsafe even talking to them. They would nod and gesture at his request, and sometimes they would lower the volume for a few hours, but it would then resume.

One night, Phil had enough! He stormed over there around 2am, and, because he was furious, and sleep deprived, he communicated in a way quite unlike his usual mild-mannered self. He banged loudly on their door, and when they opened it, he puffed himself up and crossed his arms. Then, he let rip with a string of expletives. He yelled, and he berated them for being selfish, and he told them in no uncertain terms what he would do if they did not turn their music down.

Those big, burly blokes backed right down. They turned their music off, drove their cars back into the garage, and humbly asked Phil to let them know if they ever made too much noise again. They even gave Phil their phone number so he could call and do this if needed. They apologised for the problems they had caused his entire family.

why was Phil's behaviour so effective?

Because he placed himself in rapport with them. It's that simple. Those blokes did not understand mild-mannered requests for assistance. They possibly perceived that behaviour as "wussy". **They did see and get when someone looked like them, behaved like them, and spoke like them.** They saw and heard and got him, and they responded. They treated him like one of their tribe, because now they saw him as one.

We're not saying you should go around yelling at big, burly, tattooed blokes. What we are saying is this: it is *vital*, for effective communication, that you gain and maintain rapport, no matter how unusual the other person's behaviour may seem to you, no matter how different it is to your usual behaviour. **Mirror someone: their body language, their spoken language, their written language, and you open the channels for effective, confident communication.**

how you can use communication to diffuse a tense situation

When someone is in conflict, as soon as you communicate with them in a way which holds an intent of rapport, you easily diffuse the tense situation. How do you do this? You observe their body language...then you "mirror" it. You listen to their words. You check for specific signs of stress–and you identify their communication preference...then you speak their language.

It is practical and helpful, if you have a potential conflict situation, to know you have a way to manage any crisis elegantly and confidently. You can use the key phrases below to diffuse the situation, and let the other person know that you understand where they are coming from.

For a **visual communicator** you need to let them know that *you <u>see</u> what they are saying*. For an **auditory** communicator, let them know that *you <u>hear</u> what they are saying*. For a **kinesthetic** communicator you could let them know that *you <u>get</u> what they are saying*. For a data-digital preference it's important to them that *you <u>understand</u> what they are saying*.

If someone is upset, the fastest way to gain rapport with them is to repeat the above phrases, and watch or listen for signs that the person has *seen*, *heard*, *got* or *understood* you. You will see a recognition or even gratefulness in their eyes, you will hear them slow down and change their tone, you will feel a shift in their attitude, or you'll know they've understood you.

You will then have an opportunity to "speak their language" back to them, and assist them in creating a win-win situation. This simple and profound technique can instantly shut down aggressive behaviour, and open-up effective, confident communication.

It's a particularly useful tool for coaches, parents, teachers and managers. It's simple, it's easy, and it can even be fun.

chapter 15 email secrets –
how to write the right way

why it matters
Emails are still an important component of communication, particularly in business. In this section, we are going to unveil the secrets to effective and confident communication via email. You are going to see, hear, learn and understand how to apply your "mirroring" skills, and your new awareness of the four different languages spoken by communicators.

how email secrets helped us
We have seen, heard and found this technique incredibly successful in terms of creating rapport with potential clients. After only one email exchange with a client, where Kathryn mirrored exactly the layout of the email and used some key words, she discovered in her reply that her client called her "Kath".

"Kath" is used by Kathryn's closest friends and she never introduces herself by that name, preferring to use the more formal Kathryn. So why did her client do this? Because of the rapport which had been created, she already perceived Kathryn as someone she knew well, "speaking" to her as if they were old friends.

how email secrets helped others
Tom, a manager with a data digital preference used to write emails that were perceived by his team to be abrupt and rude. The whole team learned about communication preferences and how they write different types of emails. Once Tom realised how

his emails were being received, he made simple changes to engage his team and keep rapport. At the same time, his team learned that if they receive an "abrupt" email it was simply Tom going into his data-digital mode and that the best way to respond was to mirror it.

here's the secret...

Everyone has their own unique way of writing and setting out emails. This includes their layout, sign offs, font type and size, punctuation usage and other significant features. Some people write long emails and run the words together, barely using indents or paragraphs. Others write short succinct emails. Consciously, we are not aware of what we do; we just do it.

secret number 1: body (of the email)

You can build rapport by **"mirroring" the layout** or the **body** of someone's email. When you align your email layout with theirs, **it is like mirroring someone's body language.** The layout becomes like the person's physical body that you are mirroring. Just as you mirror someone's physical gestures, in an email you can mirror:

- **Formatting** including paragraphing, spacing and format
- **Salutation** (greeting)
- **Sign off,** including signature
- **Font** type and size
- **Punctuation**

secret number 2: words

You can also **mirror the key words** they use when replying to them. In an email, you do not have body language or voice (tone, volume, pitch, pauses) to mirror, which is 93% of our communication. Thus, the words people use become of primary importance.

how to apply the secrets of effective email communication

Put on the hat of the "observer". Notice how the sender has laid out their email. Have they defined paragraphs, or run the words together? How have they signed off? What words have they used consistently? Visual language? Data-digital words?

As you reply to an email, mirror the email's:

1. Salutation & sign-off: Have they begun their email with "Hello" or "Hi" or "Dear" or "Howdy"? How have they ended it? Did they sign off with "Kind regards" or "Talk to you soon", or have they omitted a sign off, simply putting their name or initial i.e "Mark" "M" or even nothing at all? Mirror these salutations or sign-offs back to them. Mirror them precisely.

2. Words: mentally highlight key words and phrases they have used, and use them in your return email. If they've said, *'I want to **show** you **the document** I'm working on'*, reply with *'Thank you for **showing** me **the document** you're working on.'* If they've written, 'Here is the **information** I promised', answer with, 'Thank you for the **information** you promised' or even 'I've examined the **information** you emailed me...'.

3. Layout and body of email: Look at their email. How have they laid it out? Is there a comma after their salutation?

Dear Beth,

If there is a comma, include one when you write your salutation. If there isn't one, omit it.

Do the words run together with no paragraphs or indent? Mirror this back to them...even if it's not your natural way of writing an email. Even if you find the layout messy and disorganised. Even if you shudder as you do it. Do it anyway! Why? Because you are mirroring them and placing yourself in rapport.

Mirror their layout, the way the words are set out, or run together, as well as the number of spaces they leave between lines. Mirror their punctuation. If they use an exclamation mark, use one. (Visual communicators tend to use these to show you they are happy or excited.) If they don't include one, avoid it. If they have a comma after their sign-off and before their name...

Kind regards,
Beth

...do the same, even if your usual sign-off looks different to that.

Mirror any added extras. If they use an emoticon, use one. If they don't use an emoticon, do not use one. If they include a signature, include one too.

spelchekking aka spellchecking

We all know to spell-check before sending off an email. And it goes without saying—but we are going to say it anyway, as we have been asked it during many a seminar—it is ***not*** appropriate or necessary in a business context to mirror someone's spelling errors. Simply use the correct spelling in your reply email. The sender may or may not notice.

In a personal email, different rules may apply, particularly if the sender is significantly younger than you and commonly uses slang and abbreviation. In this situation, mirroring their words back to them can help you gain rapport. We'd strongly suggest you never risk it in a business context, though.

it's so obvious, they will see what I'm doing

It's possible that you will think it is so obvious, they will know what you are doing.

It's possible that you will think it is so obvious, they will know what you are doing.

It's possible that you will think it is so obvious, they will know what you are doing.

Trust us. They won't. Unless they've read this book of course, and then they'll be so happy someone else is making an effort to build rapport, you'll have instant rapport with them from that point forward.

Now, that's a win-win.

email examples of the four communication preferences

Identify the communication preferences in each of these sample emails. Answers are below.

1. To: b.bailey@pacnet.com
   From: jjones@blt.com

Hello Beth,

Great to hear from you. Thanks for the proposal. It sounds great. Would love to talk with you further about the costs so that we can tune into them more closely.

Hear from you soon,

Jeremy Jones

This communication preference is…?

2. To: b.bailey@pacnet.com
   From: jjones@blt.com

Hi Beth,

Great to see you the other day! Thanks for showing me the proposal.

It looks great and is very clear and easy to follow! Would appreciate you showing us a further break-up of the costs. Want to clearly see the vision of this proposal!

See you soon, ☺

Jeremy Jones

This communication preference is…?

3. To: b.bailey@pacnet.com
    From: jjones@blt.com

Hi Beth, How are you? Thanks for giving me the proposal. When you get a chance, could you please send me a further break-up of the costs so that our team can get a grasp on them. I will enjoy meeting with you again after that, so that I can share with you people's feelings in relation to the changes. Things are going great and we are really happy to have your support here. Thanks again Beth. Warmest Regards, Jeremy

This communication preference is…?

4. To: b.bailey@pacnet.com
    From: jjones@blt.com

Received your information re proposal.

Please indicate further details of cost for our examination.

JJ

Jeremy Jones

Director, BLT Inc.

This communication preference is...?

Answers: 1. Auditory 2. Visual 3. Kinesthetic 4. Data digital

how you can reply for maximum communication

1. The Visual Communicator's Typical Email

Hi Beth,

Great to see you the other day! Thanks for showing me the proposal.

It looks great and is very clear and easy to follow! Would appreciate you showing us a further break-up of the costs. Want to clearly see the vision of this proposal!

See you soon,

Jeremy Jones ☺

    A visual communicator will be aware of how their email looks. They often use colour, pictures, pretty background and 'emoticons' e.g ☺. In the workplace they need to be aware of making their emails look appropriately professional, as others might judge them as being shallow or frivolous, when they are simply wanting it to look nice.

    Visual communicators tend to use a lot of exclamation marks, as this communicates excitement and action!

    Their choice of words and sign-off will reflect their preference e.g "looks", "vision" and of course, *'See you soon'*. When replying, mirror their layout and the key words they have used, particularly the sign off.

It doesn't matter if you won't literally be seeing them, especially if they're on the other side of the world. Using the phrase *'See you soon'* will *show* them you *see* who *they* are.

example of a reply to a visual email

Hi Jeremy,

Great to see your email re the proposal.

Glad it's all clear and easy to follow! When can we meet face-to-face so I can show you a further break-up of the costs? So happy you see the vision of this proposal!

See you soon,

Beth Bailey ☺

2. The Auditory Communicator's Typical Email

Hello Beth
Great to hear from you. Thanks for the proposal. It sounds great. Would love to talk with you further about the costs so that we can tune into them more closely.

Hear from you soon...
Jeremy Jones

An auditory communicator will be aware of the "tone" of their email, so it tends to read well and flow smoothly. Like music. Their choice of words and sign off will reflect their communication preference; such as "sounds", "tune into" and of course, *'Hear from you soon'*.

When replying, mirror their layout, the key words they have used and the sign off, as closely as appropriate. It doesn't matter if you won't literally be speaking to them—using the phrase *'Hear from you soon'* will 'speak their language' to them.

example of a reply to an auditory email
Hello Jeremy
Great to hear from you. Thanks for your feedback re the proposal. I have some time tomorrow afternoon to discuss things further. Can you call me at the office on 012 345 6789 after 1pm?

Hear from you then...,
  Beth

3. The Kinesthetic Communicator's Typical Email

Hi Beth, How are you? Thanks for giving me the proposal. When you get a chance, could you please send me a further break-up of the costs so that our team can get a grasp on them. I will enjoy meeting with you again after that, so that I can share with you people's feelings in relation to the changes. Things are going great and we are really happy to have your support here. Thanks again Beth. Warmest Regards, Jeremy

A kinesthetic communicator will be aware of how their email makes you feel. They usually ask how you are–it feels rude for them to launch straight into any situation without asking this first. Do take the time to reply to their question; even a brief, *'I'm great thanks. How are you?'* will suffice to maintain rapport.

Their emails can tend to be long and lengthy and flowing and ongoing. In the workplace, they need to be aware of keeping their emails brief and to the point, particularly when communicating with a data-digital communicator. Otherwise busy people can become frustrated, causing them to dismiss important emails as they didn't have time to read them.

If you are a kinesthetic communicator, it's also important for you to minimise kinesthetic- feelings-based language, as it is not always appropriate in the workplace. We have seen intelligent kinesthetics, particularly females, being judged as being "flaky" or "too warm and fuzzy" simply because they used words of their preference.

A kinesthetic communicator's choice of words and sign-off will reflect their preference e.g "share", "feelings" and of course *'Warmest regards'*. And, as mentioned, do take the time to ask how they are, or even a family member if you know of one e.g *'Hope your children are well'*. They greatly appreciate it–and it will immediately place you in rapport.

example of a reply to a kinesthetic email

Hi Jeremy, How are you? Thanks for your reply re the proposal. When you get a chance, you may like to open the attached document. It's a further break-up of the costs for you and your team. I will enjoy meeting with you again soon, so that we can share your people's feelings in relation to the changes. Glad things are going great. Thanks again Jeremy. Warmest Regards, Beth

4. The Data-digital Communicator's Typical Email

Received your information re proposal.

Please indicate further details of cost for our examination.

JJ

Jeremy Jones
Director, BLT Inc. B. Eng. (Hons) M.Sc.Eng

A data-digital communicator will write an email that is brief and to the point. It will tend to contain details and data. Sometimes their emails can come across as terse, cold or unfriendly, which can be misinterpreted by other communication preferences. Kinesthetic and Auditory communicators can become the most offended by this, and, on many occasions, this behaviour has been interpreted in the workplace as one colleague thinking another colleague is upset with them when they are not.

Data-digital communicators may even omit a salutation, and if they do use one, it is usually just a name, with no preceding endearments such as "Dear ___" or "Hello". Unlike the kinesthetic communicator, they don't usually ask how you are, as it seems a waste of time or irrelevant for them to do this.

They commonly omit a sign-off, or only include their name or initial. They just want to exchange information, so they can get the job done. In the workplace it's important for them to consider adding "social niceties" e.g greetings into their emails, particularly when working with kinesthetic communicators.

In a data-digital communicator's email, their choice of words will reflect their preference e.g: "process", "procedure" and *'my understanding is'*. Their sign-off is brief and they often abbreviate their name to initials e.g 'JJ".

They are also known to include their title and qualifications, because this information—how qualified someone is—is important to them, and so they want to communicate this to you. When replying to this type of email it is appropriate to include your qualifications and title.

example of a reply to a data-digital email

Further details of cost for your examination are attached.

Please get back to me with any questions.

BB

Beth Bailey
Director, LP Pty Ltd. B.App.Sci. MBA. GAICD

why doing this is important

Remember the most important thing in being a confident communicator is to have rapport. You gain and maintain rapport when you mirror someone's email back to them. When you are in rapport with someone there is an easy agreeance, opportunities flow, and win-win outcomes are achieved.

when we mirror people's emails, rapport is achieved

It may seem like an effort, yet it takes only five seconds longer to observe an email layout and key words, then use them in your reply. What this does to the receiver, your colleague, is incredibly powerful, and subsequently what it will give and do for you is profound. This technique can also be applied to other forms of print such as letters and SMS, even Facebook postings. We do suggest SMS be used with caution, especially at the start of a new business relationship; it lends itself to too many miscommunications. However, a simple mirrored response to an SMS advising a time or venue change can assist in gaining and maintaining rapport for effective and confident communication.

chapter 16   um, er, maybe –
how to make fast, easy decisions and why you already know how to

Trust your choices, and everything is possible.
Cherie Carter-Scott, Author and Motivational Author

decisions, decisions, decisions

From the moment we awake in the morning, to last thing at night, we spend our time making decisions. This includes decisions about what we eat, wear, say or don't say, do or don't do. This is filtered through what we call our **Decision-Making Filter (DMF).**

Have you ever had so many decisions to make, that it felt, looked or sounded as if you were being overwhelmed with too much information. When you identify and use your DMF, it allows you to make decisions quickly and easily and with peace of mind, knowing that you have made the "right" decision for you at that time. You can use this DMF to help you in the areas of Health, Relationships, Career and even to discover your life passion and purpose.

We all experience the world through seeing, hearing, feeling and facts & figures, however we have a preference for one of these over the others.

Recall a significant decision you made recently which you...
- ✓ Made totally on your own (no opinions from others) and
- ✓ Were happy with the outcome of

Examples of decisions might involve a job, relationship, car, or a less significant decision such as buying a new suit or upgrading a laptop.

As you recall that decision, ask yourself:
Did you <u>primarily</u> make that decision, because...

- It **looked** right to you?
- It **sounded** right to you?
- It **felt** right to you?
- It made **sense**/was **logical**?

Identifying this will give you your preference in terms of which way of decision making is right for you. Go with this decision. Of course, if you are buying an expensive item such as a house, for most people, price must be a consideration. However, for some people, even if the price was right, it would still have to look good or feel right for them to buy it. You may have heard someone say, *'I wouldn't do that job if you paid me a million dollars a year!'* This is because it feels wrong to them or it looks wrong, or even sounds wrong.

You may have one or more preference coming into play during times of decision-making, as your preference combinations are activated. Perhaps it looks right and feels right. Maybe, for you it must add up and sound right.

Alternately, if we have made a decision in the past which we are *not* happy with, it is usually because we have not attended or listened to our DMF. Maybe the outcome was logical, yet it felt wrong, and you did it anyway.

how using a DMF helped others

Sometimes, something can appear to be okay when it's not. Suppose you were buying a second-hand car from a private seller. Maybe that car that seems to be exactly what you were looking for, and it's in your price range, yet it just doesn't feel right for you. It's possible that your DMF, is letting you know that the car has a problem even the owner doesn't know about. Or maybe there is something better just around the corner.

Jenna, a friend of ours, wanted to buy a Mazda. She did her research and test-drove a few cars. She finally located one she thought was perfect. It was the colour she wanted, had low mileage, a great music system and it felt comfortable and smelled nice. And it was in her price range. Her brother, a mechanic, checked it out for her and pronounced it *'a good deal'*.

Yet Jenna, who makes decisions based on gut feelings (kinesthetic communicator), felt uncomfortable. It all seemed to be okay yet she just got a bad feeling about it. So, she told the owner she'd think about it, and walked away from the car. Her brother thought she had made a wrong decision.

The next day, Jenna went to view another car and it was exactly what she wanted...yet it was $2000 cheaper, as the owner was travelling overseas and needed to sell it in a hurry. Jenna saved herself $2000 by listening to her inner feeling.

how using your DMF can help you

If you follow your DMF when making decisions, it leads you to the right place. It really is this simple. The only reason that decisions may have been difficult for you in the past is because you were worrying about what someone else might think or you, or were concerned about the impact of your decision on others.

There is a brilliant quote from Shakespeare's Hamlet:

'This above all: to thine own self be true; and it must follow, as the night the day; Thou canst not then be false to any man.'

'Hamlet,' Act I, Scene iii
William Shakespeare (1564 - 1616) English Dramatist & Poet

This is so true. When we are true to ourselves, we are true to everyone else. If someone makes a decision, and their heart is not in it, in effect they are lying to and dishonouring the people around them. They might think it's the best decision, but in the long run, truth is better, isn't it?

chapter 17   stand in their shoes – why you might need to do this and how to in 3 easy steps

why walk in someone else's shoes?

There is a North American Indian proverb which says, *'Don't judge a man until you have walked two moons in his moccasins'.*

Confident communicators know how to step into another person's "Model of the World" and consider other perspectives. This is akin to "stepping into their shoes". It is particularly useful during moments of conflict, as the key to effective negotiating requires finding and creating a "win-win". We can only do this when we acknowledge that there are many different perspectives which all need to be considered.

Have you ever had an unpleasant conflict with someone and you just can't let it go? This conflict may have been with your partner, your child, a parent, a business associate, or just anyone that you've had this conflict with. Or maybe you were attempting to find a solution to something that affected both of you.

The third person perspective process involves examining an issue from three perspectives: yours, the other person's and a third person perspective.

The process is outlined on the following pages. When doing this exercise, we suggest that you have someone talk you through it step by step

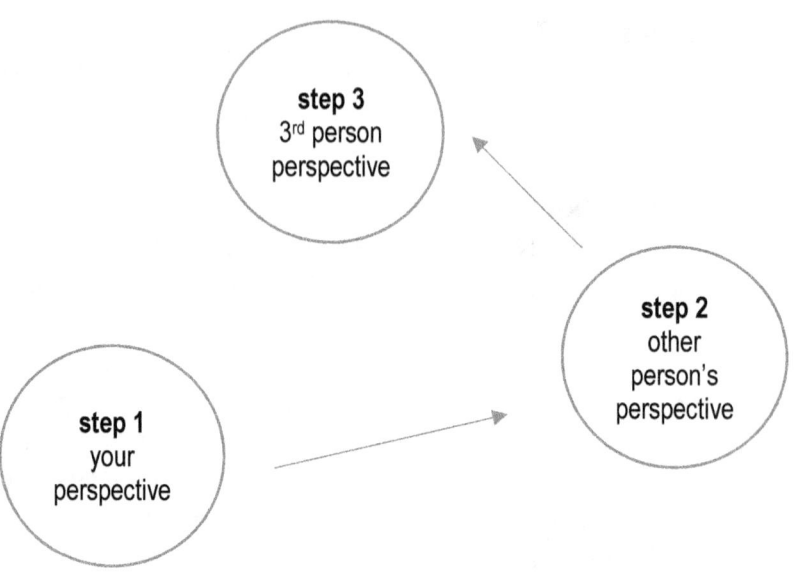

step 1   your perspective

Re-experience the situation through your own eyes. Stand up and feel what it is like and notice the other person's reactions, their physical posture, their gestures and be aware of how you are feeling, what you are seeing and hearing and the thoughts that you are thinking. Now, clear this image away and step to where the other person is.

step 2   other person's perspective

Now re-experience the situation as the other person. Use the information that you gathered in the first stage. Step into their shoes and as you progress through the experience, imagine what their feelings and attitudes are, what's happening for them, what are they seeing and hearing and thinking? Fantastic. Yes, we know this is not easy to do, and you do know this. Then shake your arms, hands, legs and feet, to shake it out of your body.

step 3   third person perspective

The third step is a detached, third person perspective. So now step away from where those two people are and imagine looking at the two people. Imagine you're both there, watching them from a neutral space, and be aware of any new information that is being gathered by this perspective. What can you see? What can you feel between the two? What are you hearing and what are you thinking about that interaction as it is going on?

okay, now what?

The information you've gathered has enormous value. You can now perceive how others see you, and how an entire situation can be viewed from a neutral position. So instead of having only one way of experiencing the world, which is your way, you now have three ways: you have **yours**, **theirs**, which enables you to have empathy as you gain new understanding, and you also have **the third person perspective,** which is **neutral** and **disassociated**.

Having this extra information can allow you to gain a fuller insight into what went on. It allows you to reframe any situation and expand your perspective of it. This technique also enables you to find a solution that becomes a way for both of you to 'win' in the situation.

chapter 18 word play –
how to use words to say what you mean and mean what you say

the power of words

Words are powerful. Words can demotivate & disempower, yet, they can also motivate and empower. This chapter can give you the words to change your mindset, your attitude and enhance your skills and talents just by changing the words you use. How?

Your subconscious mind doesn't know the difference between what you imagine and what's real; it believes whatever you tell it. By using positive self-talk you'll create your own private cheer squad–*you*. After all, everyone needs encouragement and moral support.

how word play helped us

As an executive coach Carol is very careful when she sets tasks for her clients. It is very easy to ask them to ***try*** to get the tasks done before she sees them again. Now that she knows the power of words and how they impact on performance, and how the word "try" is actually an inaction word, she now phrases her requests much differently. *'It's possible you will enjoy doing this and have it completed by our next meeting'* versus *'**Try** to do this before our next meeting'*

how word play helped others

We had a client who needed to communicate to the local community some changes which needed to happen for the benefit of the community. The team would go into community forums saying, *'You will like what we're about to propose'*. The problem with this statement is that immediately there were people who objected: *'How do you know what I am thinking?'"*

They have now changed their language to **'It's possible that** *you'll really like what we're about to propose.'* This language receives much less resistance and their message is more likely to be considered'.

how word play can help you

We are going to show, tell and give you information to:
- ✓ Avoid words that discourage and de-motivate
- ✓ Use words that motivate and empower
- ✓ Focus on what you want
- ✓ Rephrase for maximize impact

that's right!

Using the phrase *'That's right'* reassures someone's subconscious mind you are listening to them, seeing who they are and receiving the information they are giving you. *'That's right'* maintains rapport, something that confident communicators know is vital to effective communication.

This phrase is useful in a workplace meeting, particularly when there are several people holding different perspectives. An example of this might be if someone in a meeting offered a point of view which you disagree with. They might say something like, *'We should make it office policy that everyone has to wear casual clothes on a Friday.'*

Your response could be, *'That's right. And perhaps we could also offer everyone a choice to wear casual or not depending on the meetings they have that day.'*

This maintains agreeance with their subconscious mind, whilst enabling your opinion to be heard. It means they are much more likely to consider your opinion, and you are most likely to stay in rapport with them.

it's possible that...

This clever little phrase opens us up to possibility. There are always infinite solutions...when we sit in our comfort zone, maybe we haven't been able to hear, get or see these solutions because the possibilities were outside our comfort zone, until someone focussed us on them. *'It's possible that...'* is a statement you can't argue with.

It's possible that Elvis is alive.
It's possible that UFOs exist.
It's possible that you will remember everything from this book and use it straight away to have an impact in your life.

It is difficult to disagree with these comments. Regardless of your opinion about Elvis or UFO's or your infinite and brilliant learning capacity, you can see, hear, get and process how the possibility does exist.

Kathryn enjoys using this phrase when she finds herself in controversial conversations. You know the type; those involving the three topics some people say you should never discuss: religion, politics and sex. She had a recent conversation about same sex marriage with someone who insisted that, *'Marriage is between a man and a woman'*. Her gentle reply was, 'Yes, and it's possible that marriage, as an institution which is always growing and changing, can change with the demands of society.'

Because she knew this was someone particularly influenced by the limitations of the media, she added, *'It's also possible we don't always hear and get all sides of the debate. It's possible there is more to the rights of same-sex marriage than maybe we know.'*

Interestingly, when presented with possibility, this rather opinionated and dogmatic listener appeared to be considering her opinion.

negatives

The subconscious mind does **_not_** process negatives. If we say to you, 'Do *not* think of a purple frog' what do you think of? That's right, a purple frog–the very thing we said to **_not_** think of! The mind cannot process negatives as they are intangible words.

If you say to a child, *'Don't run!'* their subconscious mind hears *'Run'*. And that's exactly what they do!

If you say to someone, *'Don't worry.'* Their subconscious mind processes that message as, *'Do worry.'*

If you say to a client, *'Don't worry. We're handling that issue.'* Their subconscious mind actually hears, *'Do worry. We're handling the issue.'* This is a mixed message.

To have clear and concise communication say what you **do** want to leave the person with, rather than what you don't.

If you want to be clear and confident in all your communication, we suggest you seriously consider making the new language in the following examples a permanent part of your vocabulary. The easiest way to do this is make one phrase a focus each week. You could even put the phrase next to your computer at work, near the telephone, even on the bathroom mirror. This can remind you to use the more empowering language.

how not using negatives helped others

As ex-school teachers, we know first-hand the frustration of giving directions which are dismissed or disobeyed. Many times a day, teachers direct their students to do certain things. If they are unaware of the power of their words, they may spend their days directing children to do the very opposite of what they need or want them to do.

We've seen teachers rename their list of classroom rules to support this concept. *'Don't forget your belongings'* became *'Remember all your belongings'*. *'Don't run in the classroom'* became *'Walk in the classroom'*.

Here are a few examples with suggestions to replace them:

common phrase	replace with
Don't forget …	Remember…
Don't run.	Walk.
Don't make noise.	Please be quiet.
Don't worry.	That's fine.
No worries.	Happy to help.
I'm not concerned about that.	I'm happy with that.
It doesn't mean…	It means…

but…but…but

When we use the word "but", it negates all that has been said before it.

Consider these…

I want to help you, **but** I am busy that night.
I know you work hard, **but** I work hard too.
I understand what you are saying, **but** what I think is…

Now, instead of using the word **but**, replace it with **and**.

Consider these…

I want to help you **and** I am busy that night.
I know you work hard **and** I work hard too.
I understand what you are saying, **and** I also think …

how butting out helped others

You can find and implement innovative and fun methods of remembering to replace "but" with "and". One of our clients, a creative team in the fashion industry, called us in to work with their team. Their manager said it was because they were becoming negative in their interactions,

When we listened to their language and observed them in action, we heard them using the word "but" quite commonly. In fact, their usage was so regular, where some people use a "swear jar" they could have used a "but jar".

When we pointed out their overuse of the word, they found it fascinating. Most people who work in creative fields are familiar with the power of allowing creative thought to flow. They are also aware of what shuts down creativity. Yet, that little creature known as "but" had crept its way into this workplace, and it acted as a huge obstruction, stopping creative flow in its tracks.

Once they realised what had occurred, this extremely creative team devised a clever solution: they placed a picture of a cigarette butt in their lunchroom and brainstorming spaces. It had the words *Replace "but" with "and"* underneath the picture. Each time they saw it, they remembered to replace "but" with "and"... and a positive and vital creative flow recommenced, making their workplace once again a happy and constructive one.

Remember that rapport is vital to effective communication and to keeping the lines of communication open. When we use "but", we put ourselves out of rapport with the person we say it to. When we use "and", we keep ourselves in rapport by maintaining agreeance.

should

Read these statements. As you are reading them, check how they feel, look and sound to you.

You should do that.
You should know that.

Does this make you feel bad, perhaps even like a little kid who has done something wrong? **Should** is a controlling word and it can bring up people's insecurities and baggage. A statement like *'You should know that'* can imply someone is stupid, even if we believe they are intelligent.

Instead of using *should*, replace it with *could*.

Read these statements. As you are reading them, check how they feel, look and sound to you.

You could do that.
You could know that…

Could looks, sounds and feels much more empowering, doesn't it? When you replace the word "should" with "could", you maintain rapport and have confident communication.

try

There's an infamous line from Star Wars where Yoda says to Luke Skywalker, *'Try or Try Not. Do or do not. There is no try.'* Do this exercise. Put a pen on the table in front of you. Now ***try*** to pick up the pen. If you picked it up, you didn't *try* to pick it up, you actually did pick it up!

"Try" is a "nothing" word. In fact, *try* gives people an out if they don't want to do something. How many times have you asked someone to do something for you and their response is *'I'll try'*? What they are really saying is, "*I might do it*".

Here are some examples:

Manager: *Can you get that report done by Friday?*
Colleague: *I'll try.*

Mother: *Please put out the rubbish bin tonight.*
Son: *I'll try, Mum.*

When someone says, *'I'll try'*, it covers them and often gets people off their back. But it also causes frustration in others.

It's far better to say, *'I will do it'* or *'Friday is too soon however I will have it done by next Tuesday.'*

There are several phrases which are a variation on the phrase "I'll try" and they also communicate the concept of "trying". We suggest you avoid using these phrases.

They include:

I'll do my best.
I'll give it a go.
I'll attempt it.

Rather than use "try", or any of the variations above, be honest and direct in your communication. If you can't get something completed by a certain date, or have no intention of doing it at all, communicate that. If you can do it then say '*I'll do it*'.

chapter 19 metaprograms matter – what they are and why you need to use them

why you need to use metaprograms

We talked earlier of how you gather information from the world. We gave you a diagram showing how, out of approximately two million bits of information surrounding you, you are only *consciously* aware of around 134 bits per second (bps).

Given the abundance of information we are inundated with, at both a conscious and subconscious level, we need a filtering system. If we had to process all of it at once, our brains might possibly overload, explode or implode. So, our mind contains a filter called the "Reticular Activating System" or "R.A.S", and it filters this information for us. **The four communication preferences are only one of a staggering <u>one hundred and thirty-five filters</u>.** We have given you comprehensive information on this filter, as applying that knowledge is one of the fastest ways to effective and confident communication.

There are five more secrets to confident communication, and these are revealed from within these set of filters known as metaprograms.

You have observed and mirrored body language; you have used key words and phrases in your communication. You have done the same in your email. Yet you still may have issues with that one key person. You need to communicate with them more effectively. You need to communicate with them more confidently. You've applied all the tools. Yet, when it comes to the crunch, you can't seem to communicate your message in the way you want.

Maybe you're ready to make a key decision and you require someone else's input or signoff? But they're taking too long, or worse they won't decide at all. And you can't seem to convince them to make one! You are frustrated and annoyed, and you are trying to be a confident communicator, but they're not listening to you, seeing you or hearing your information.

Perhaps you're searching for new ways to motivate your team? You've gained and maintained rapport, you're speaking their language, yet when it comes to "motivation hour" you look, sound and feel like a fraud. You are motivating them in a way which works for you, but it's not working for them. Or possibly, most of the team seems motivated. But there's someone in your team who you can't seem to crack! Is it their fault…or yours?

If you want to see, hear, get and understand another layer to being a confident communicator, then read on.

what are metaprograms?

Metaprograms are programs which govern our behaviour. They are filters we run subconsciously, which influence our ability to make decisions, motivate ourselves and others, and manage people and events more effectively in our world.

The concept of "metaprograms" was introduced by Carl Jung– the founder of analytical psychology. The Myer-Briggs Personality Indicators identify four basic metaprograms.

These are **External Behaviour** (Introvert/Extrovert), our **Internal Process** (Intuitor/Sensor), our **Internal State** (Thinker/Feeler) and our **Adaptive Response** (Judger/Perceiver). Most people are familiar with Myer-Briggs, so we will not address those indicators here. We will instead focus on other metaprograms, which we have found valuable in avoiding and maintaining confident communication.

The term "metaprogram" comes from the Greek words *meta* meaning **"with, across, or after"**, and *program* from *prographein* meaning **"written publicly"**. Metaprograms cover or run *across* our entire communication, in spoken and written form. With our metaprograms, we declare ourselves publicly, we communicate how we receive information, and what pieces of data we filter in and out, and why.

Put simply, **metaprograms are filters we run.** We filter information in and out, based on our subconscious mind directives (our beliefs, our stories). As with the four communication preferences, bringing them to conscious awareness assists us. Seeing, hearing and receiving information on how we decide what we do, causes us to be more consciously effective in our communication. This, in turn, enables us to be more confident in the entirety of our communication.

metaprograms = increased perception = confident communication

The four communication preferences: visual, auditory, kinesthetic, and data-digital are one of the metaprograms. They are a filter we run, determining how we receive information from our world via our five senses. There are numerous metaprograms which you can discover via research. We also suggest you read *Time Line Therapy and the Basis of Personality* (James, T and Woodsmall, W, Crown House Publishing Ltd, 2017) for a more comprehensive study of metaprograms.

We have narrowed this list of one hundred and thirty-five down to five metaprograms. These programs often emerge when avoiding poor communication and clarifying confident communication. Whilst they are brilliant in their simplicity, and effective in their implementation, our clients rarely report having encountered them. Yet the results, when applied, are truly magical in increasing confident communication.

So, we wanted to share this often secret, yet powerful knowledge with you. As you learn them, you may see, hear or experience a familiarity with the information. This is because you use and run these filters every day at a *subconscious* level. Just as with the four communication preferences, we are bringing them to your *conscious* awareness. This enables you to apply them now for effective, confident communication.

what are the five secret metaprograms?

The five secret metaprograms are:

1. Motivation filter
2. Convincer filter
3. Feedback filter
4. Speaking filter
5. Listening filter

secret metaprogram 1: motivate, motivate, motivate

The first metaprogram is our **motivation filter.** This is how we are inspired to do or not do something, our incentive, what drives us towards our goals or away from those things we do not want.

This filter is often referred to as **"the stick"** or **"the carrot"**. Some people are motivated by "the stick"–by the threat of something painful occurring which they don't desire, such as losing a job or a race, or being poor. In psychology, we refer to this group of people as **"away from motivators"**.

Other people are motivated by "the carrot", by the possibility of something occurring which they desire, such as a gold medal, owning their own home or getting married. We refer to these people as **"towards motivators"**.

Motivation filters are commonly used in advertising. Some advertisers use strong "away from" motivation, such as a stop smoking advertisement showing someone dying, or a "driver safety" promotion displaying a car crash. Other advertisements contain "towards" motivation, such as lottery ads featuring all the things and experiences you can buy when you win millions of dollars.

The most effective advertisements contain some "towards" motivation and some "away from" motivation.

Many people are not simply one or the other. As with the four communication preferences, some people can be a mix of these two filters, and will sit somewhere along a continuum. For example, Carol is an "away from" motivator with a little bit of "towards". If you need to motivate a group of people, include both "towards" and "away from" language, to avoid placing yourself out of rapport, and to ensure effective and confident communication.

"the stick"	"the carrot"

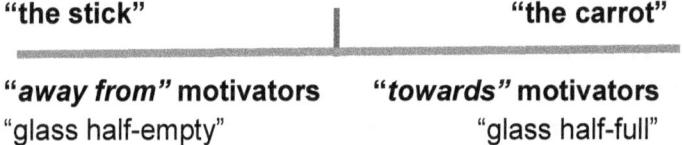

| *"away from"* motivators | *"towards"* motivators |
| "glass half-empty" | "glass half-full" |

When we teach this to clients, it's interesting how often people refer to the **"away from"** filter as **"negative"** and the **"towards"** filter as **"positive".** Using this language, places a judgement around our preferences. It is akin to saying a "visual communicator" is better than a "data-digital" one. They are simply filters.

So why do some of us go into judgement around "good" and "bad" or "positive" and "negative" filters? It's because **most of us have been programmed within a "positive psychology" world.** We've been trained to think of what we are moving towards as "being positive" and to set our goals this way.

Traditional goal setting strategies, *tell me what you want; imagine having that; set a goal around it; take necessary action; achieve your goal,* **are designed for "towards" motivators.** We're taught to be *positive, positive, positive!* We're taught to "reframe", and to refer to a "problem" as a "challenge". And we'd certainly expect a motivational speaker or coach to be "positive" in their language, and speak of achieving the positive, tangible things people commonly desire. Yet **someone who understands true motivation, knows that people are motivated in different ways.**

Some people possess this knowledge innately; it can be what separates a good manager or coach from an excellent one. Often, they don't know *how* they are motivating people, they simply know that what they do works. Fortunately, researchers have observed and identified the specific strategies for motivation. We have learned these, so can teach them to you. If you want to motivate yourself and others, for confident communication, you need to discern what's happening inside another person's model of the world, so you can avoid the pitfalls, and meet their needs.

how using this filter helped us motivate a team

When Carol learned about motivation filters, she recalled a story from her childhood as a young swimmer. As she and her younger sister were close in age, they swam in the same grouped-age races. She recalls her coach pulling them both aside before the first race. To Michelle, who has always been a glass-half-full person, he suggested—in a warm and light-hearted tone, 'Now, Michelle, when you are racing today, I want you to swim your best. Go really hard and you'll win that gold medal!' Carol remembers rolling her eyes as he spoke to Michelle, because what she heard sounded so "fluffy" and "sappy" to her ears. It would not have motivated her; it would have simply annoyed her!

Then the coach turned to Carol, pointed his finger sternly, and said, 'And you Carol, I will kick your ass from here to kingdom come if you don't win!' As a mostly "away from" motivator, this was the perfect motivation for her.

how using this filter helped motivate others

The Australian culture in which we've grown up, is mostly motivated by "towards" concepts. When Carol worked with the Australian Swim Team, her motivational language was mainly "towards":

When you do this, you'll achieve your best,
This can help you win.
This helps you obtain what you want.

When Carol worked with the British Swim Team, by contrast, she discovered them to be, as a culture, motivated more by "away from" language:

When you do this, you won't have to train harder.
This can help you avoid losing.
This helps you prevent disappointment.

Being able to speak their language, motivated both teams in the most efficient way possible.

Cultures around the world will differ in the way they are motivated. As teachers, we observed many students interacting with their parents. Consistently, we noted parents of immigrant children, possessing a different motivation filter to the parents who had grown up in Australia.

Generally, those parents who had travelled from another country to Australia, because of war, poverty or simply the promise of a more prosperous life, were **moving away from** something they did not want. They were "away from" motivators, or their circumstances helped create that. Extreme emotional situations, such as having to leave your home to stay safe, tend to form stronger motivation responses within our neural networks.

Their children, on the other hand, had been born here, or were so young when they arrived, they had no conscious recall of their homeland. They did not need to move away from anything painful or difficult in the way their parents had, so they adopted the motivational strategies of their new country: **towards** motivation.

When these children interacted with their parents, tension often arose. Children complained that their parents were often telling them:

*If you don't work hard at school, you won't get a good job.
If you don't get a good job, you won't be successful in life.
If you fail, you'll shame the family.*

These are "away from" motivational statements, and they did **_not_** motivate our students, merely caused them to feel angry and frustrated.

Instead, they needed to hear "towards" motivation:

*When you work hard at school, you'll get good marks and it's possible you may even top the class.
The better your marks, the more choice you'll have in life- to be, do and have anything you want!
When you do well, I feel so proud of you.*

When they were communicated to in this way, their faces lit up, they sounded happier and felt excited about their futures.

how to elicit the motivation filter

To determine your own or another's motivation filter, ask: **What's important to you about a job/car/relationship?**

Let's use a car as an example. Suppose you ask someone, *'What's important to you about a car...?'*

An "away from" motivator might reply:
*It doesn't break down.
It's not noisy.*

It's not expensive.

A "<u>towards</u>" motivator, might answer:
It is reliable.
It runs quietly.
It's affordable.

As you read these examples now, it's possible it may look, sound and feel as if we are simply playing with words, yet remember how you have learned that **the language people use matters.** When you speak to a visual communicator, using visual words, you are speaking their language. In the same way, when you speak to an "away from" motivator or a "towards motivator" in their language, they will respond. The language they use shows, tells and gives you the motivation filter they are running.

Once you know their filter, you can avoid someone being unmotivated, as you confidently give them information in a way they can see, hear and understand.

how using this filter helps you motivate others

the "<u>away from</u>" motivator at a glance:
characteristics:
- ✓ Move away from what they don't want
- ✓ Energised by pain/deadlines/problems
- ✓ Good at trouble shooting
- ✓ Can have trouble staying on track if distracted by problems

motivating language:
- ✓ Avoid e.g 'When you do X you'll avoid Y.'
- ✓ 'Won't have to...'
- ✓ Prevent
- ✓ '...so that doesn't happen.'

the "<u>towards</u>" motivator at a glance:
characteristics:
- ✓ Excited by goals
- ✓ Outcome focussed
- ✓ Manages priorities well
- ✓ Can be naive to potential pitfalls

motivating language:
- ✓ Obtain
- ✓ Get
- ✓ Benefit
- ✓ Achieve

When motivating someone, use their motivational language. If they are an "away from" motivator, talk to them about what *won't* happen if they don't take certain action. Remind them of the pain, problems and deadlines which they might want to move away from.

If they are a "towards" motivator, talk to them about the benefits they will gain and their ideal outcomes. Dangle the carrots – their dreams and goals – in front of them, and entice them to reach for them.

It's a time waster speaking to someone in a "foreign" language. Expend your energy motivating people in the way *they* need and will respond to.

Even if it seems strange or clunky or illogical for you to motivate someone in this way, do it anyway. How come? Just as it may feel or sound strange when you first speak a foreign language, so it may seem strange to communicate in a way which is foreign to you. Yet it is the way someone else needs to be motivated.

When you don't speak a foreign language to someone, you avoid good communication.

When you give them what they need, you get what you need, in a clear and confident way.

secret metaprogram 2: I'm convinced you can be convinced

The second filter is our **convincer filter.** This filter is how we are convinced something is good, right, or right for us. It's how we know someone else is doing a good (or bad) job. It affects how quickly (or slowly) we make decisions. We run this filter when we learn. We use it when we buy, when we discern the correct path for us in life, when we make decisions.

Some people are immediately convinced. We call this an **"Automatic"** convincer filter. Other people need to compare a number of items or opportunities, such as two jobs or three cars. We call this a **"Number of times"** convincer. The third group of people require a **"Period of time"** to be convinced of something. The fourth group are **"Consistent"** convincers, which means they need convincing every single time.

how using this filter helped us

Carol has an "automatic convincer filter". Her husband has a "period of time" convincer. When they were making decisions, Carol used to become frustrated, as she was ready to buy but her husband needed to wait, allowing his "time convincer" to run its course. He would feel pressured by her need to make decisions faster than he was able. Furthermore, they would miss out on money-saving bargains or special offers, as he was not ready to take them up.

Now, she knows to plant seeds. When they wanted to take the family to Italy, she starting planning it a year in advance, knowing he would need this time to run his filter around the various decisions which needed to be made. Their trip preparation became an easy and much less frustrating event for both of them.

how using this filter helped others

When he saw and heard this information, Tim, a car salesman we know, was fascinated. He finally understood–on a deeper level–why some customers would look at his cars, then go away, before they came back to buy from him. He realised they were either "number of time" or "period of time" convincers. Some of them were going to other caryards so they could compare the cars there with those in Tim's yard. Others were allowing their "period of time" filter to elapse.

As he had learned how to elicit their filter through asking a simple question–one we'll teach you–he knew that if he maintained rapport, they were more likely to come back and buy from him. Rather than being "dirty" with them that they didn't buy–and breaking rapport–he farewelled them happily, keeping notes to remember them when they returned. His sales increased significantly.

how using the convincer filter helps you

When you see, hear, get and understand that different people have different needs to be convinced, and when you figure out what they are, it expands your world. You can teach better. You can impart information more effectively. You can manage others with ease. You can make co-decisions easily and effortlessly. You can gain and maintain greater rapport. You can avoid poor communication and communicate clearly and confidently. What used to be difficult, a struggle or downright annoying, becomes easy, simple and fun now.

how to elicit the convincer filter

The convincer filter has two parts:
1. convincer **preference** (which **_communication preference_** we use in discerning a decision or satisfying ourselves to someone's performance)
2. convincer **demonstration** filter (the _**time**_ it takes us to be convinced)

In other words, to be convinced someone is doing a good job, we'd need to know **_how_** they receive that information e.g seeing, hearing, and the **_amount of time_** it takes them to be convinced or make that decision.

Let's take a typical scenario: You've hired a new colleague, and your manager and yourself want to be convinced they are doing a good job. Firstly, ask yourself: **_How do you know when someone is good at what they do?_**

Your answer will be linked closely to your communication preference(s). If you are a visual communicator, you will need to observe your colleague's behaviour, seeing how they are doing a good job. If you're have an auditory preference, you'll want to hear about their achievements, or have them tell you of their wins. If you relate to the world through a kinesthetic communication preference, you may want to spend time with them, completing tasks together, getting a sense of their efficiency level. If you're data-digital in your preference, you may prefer to read something they've written, gather data about them and their qualifications, and possibly even implement testing in a formal or informal capacity such as self-assessment.

Secondly, take this preference of how you know someone is good at what they do, and ask yourself: **How *often* does someone have to demonstrate competency for you to be convinced?**

There are several possible answers here, and they each indicate a specific convincer demonstration filter.

Automatic:
This person will assume you will do a good job, unless you show them otherwise. It is often linked closely to a visual preference. If it looks efficient, it probably is. As they are convinced so quickly, they can become impatient with others who take longer. As this preference tends to view a more global perspective, they may miss detail missing from an employee's behaviour. And this detail may be important or relevant. When making a decision, an automatic convincer does so immediately and quickly, hiring or buying at speed. Depending on the situation, this can hold positive or negative implications.

When asked, ***How often does someone have to demonstrate competency for you to be convinced?*** their answer will be something like, ***'Straight away!'*** or *'Immediately'*.

Number of times:
This type of processor will need to experience something several times to be convinced. They will need to compare more than one option when buying or considering a choice. They may need to visit a store or venue, or meet with you two or three times in order to be convinced.

When asked, ***How often does someone have to demonstrate competency for you to be convinced?*** their answer will be something like, ***'Three times'*** or ***'two to three times'***.

To help them be convinced, you can say to them, *'It's possible after using this technique two or three times it will become really easy and effective.'*

Period of time:
This convincer strategy needs to experience competence for several days or weeks, or even months.

When asked, ***How often does someone have to demonstrate competency for you to be convinced?*** they will respond with ***'I will know in three months'*** or *'In three weeks I can give you my decision'*.

To convince them of the value of something, future pace them. Take them out into their future and ask them to **'imagine how great your life is in two or three months because you've applied these amazing confident communication skills'**.

Consistent:
This person is never convinced. They need you to prove competency to them every single time. They shine in a role where quality control is required.

When asked, *How **often** does someone have to demonstrate competency for you to be convinced?* they will respond with *'Every single time'*, *'Always'* or *'Never"*.

This can be a challenging preference for others who find their consistent filter tiring or exhausting. It can often place them out of rapport with others. We suggest you don't waste energy trying to convince them. Instead, we suggest you use a magic statement we're going to give you. This statement speaks directly to their subconscious mind, bypassing resistance, and it places the emphasis for action back on them where it belongs.

The magic statement to say to someone with a "consistent convincer filter" is, *'Only you can decide...'*

Difficulty can occur in communication when two differing convincer demonstration filters interact. An automatic processer will be ready to take action, or immediately convinced of an employee's competence. Their colleague may run a "number of times" filter, and need to see two or three demonstrations of competency, before they are convinced of their colleague's efficiency.

We run convincer filters in our relationships. We run them at work. We run them in our day-to-day decisions. When you apply this knowledge, life moves from difficult to easy, and your communication becomes increasingly confident now.

But only if that's important to you, of course.

secret metaprogram 3: I need some feedback

The third filter is our **"feedback filter"**. This filter is how we know we are doing a good job, and it's how we gather the data to prove that. Some of us do this by going outside of ourselves. We call this an **"external feedback filter"**. Others do this by going within. We call this an **"internal feedback filter"**.

Many of us use a combination of the two. Effective leaders, managers, parents and coaches usually possess an internal feedback filter, which they then supplement through checking for data outside of themselves, that is, using their external feedback filter. We call this internal with an external check.

how using this filter helped us

Kathryn was training a group of trainers in an accelerated learning program. The trainers ran the programs in satellite centres, thus needing to work independently, as they were required to manage and assess themselves.

One of the trainers reported generally struggling with her teaching. She was able to tell Kathryn how the students seemed to be experiencing the program. *'They look like they're enjoying it'* and *'A few of them have told me they've learned a lot.'* Yet when asked how she saw and felt **she** was going, she offered Kathryn a blank look. *'I don't know,'* was her response. She stared at Kathryn in bewilderment, literally unable to answer the question.

Through asking the question which we will teach you in a moment, Kathryn discovered the trainer had an "external feedback filter", but did not seem to possess an *internal* feedback filter.

This is a difficult filter to run in a teaching situation, as students do not always give you feedback, especially teenagers, which was the group she was teaching. You need to be able to know within yourself that you are on the right track, without relying solely on external information. However, people can learn to shift their filter, becoming more internal or external as their roles require.

During their weekly catch-ups, Kathryn asked leading questions to encourage this trainer to pay attention to her *internal* data. This included asking questions such as "How do you think you went today" and "How did it look through your eyes". Within a few weeks, she no longer needed Kathryn to ask these questions, as she was voluntarily reporting on internal data. As she began to pay attention to her internal feedback, her training sessions became much more effective.

This situation altered the way the company recruited further trainers. Kathryn suggested they include this question in their interview process, thus ensuring future trainers they employed possessed an "internal with an external check filter". Whilst people can be trained to shift their preference along a continuum, it was still taxing on Kathryn's time and the company assets to do this. It ensured all future trainers possessed the specific skillset needed for this job.

how using this filter helped others

When Carol and Kathryn began co-presenting their training sessions over twenty years ago, Carol's "external filter" was much higher than what it is now. Back then, when completing a workshop or seminar, Carol was sensitive to negative feedback if she received any. Perusing a pile of feedback forms, containing 99% positive comments, she would take note of the one piece of feedback she considered negative: *'The presenter did not explain the section about accountability clearly enough'.* It affected her confidence and made her feel as if her performance had not been effective, when, in reality, it had been excellent.

As we discussed this feedback, we applied the information about feedback filters. Carol asked herself questions leading her to examine and develop her "internal feedback filter" effectively leading herself along the continuum. Now, she still considers external feedback, but goes internally to validate this information. If relevant, she will make adjustments. If it is not reflective of the majority opinion, she put it into perspective.

Through observing hundreds of groups over the years, we have discovered that feedback filters vary dramatically, and this affects the delivery of information. Some groups are external in their feedback, and so, as an audience, they are more interactive and animated.

Other groups are more internal, so their processing and learning is internalised. It often depends on their profession, even their specific sport or industry.

We have found sports administrators, engineers and accountants to be highly internal in their feedback. Thus, when delivering seminar content to them, they will give little or no external feedback to the presenter or their fellow participants. We have learned to expect minimal feedback from these groups. Carol has learned to see or "read" this audience as **internal-feedback filtered people**, so she simply goes within to check on how they are receiving the information, and adjusts accordingly. This ability enables her to reach all the people in her audience, leaving no-one behind, and makes her a more effective communicator.

A group of fashion designers, by contrast, may be **external** in their processing, so they engage with the presenter and with each other in a way which is interactive, animated and externalised. From a presenter's perspective, Carol finds it easier working with these groups. She can see they are perceiving the information, and as a visual communicator with a tendency to an external check, she does not need to adjust her innate presenting style.

A crowd of coaches often sit somewhere in the middle of these two extremes, as they are trained to internalise information, and also give feedback.

how using this filter helps you

There is no "right" filter or "wrong" filter. There is no "better" filter. As with the four communication styles, there are simply preferences suited to particular filters. The important thing is to apply specific filters to the appropriate environments for confident communication. Here's how you can do this.

how to elicit the feedback filter

To elicit someone's feedback filter, ask them: **How do you know you are doing a good job?**

Someone with an **"*internal* feedback filter"** will answer:
I just know.
I have a good feeling.
It feels like the group are with me.
I am in the zone.

Someone with an **"*external* feedback filter"** will reply:
I receive a reward.
I look at the figures.
I came first in my race and achieved my PB.
I can see my team are enjoying themselves.

These are the two extremes of this filter and they sit either side of a continuum.

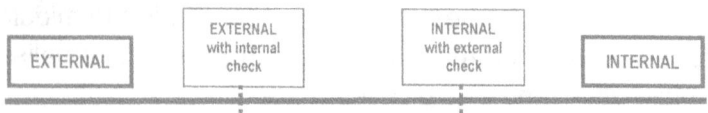

Some people's feedback filter means they check internally, then go outside of themselves for clarification. We call this filter an **"internal, with an external check"**. Others will check externally first, then go inside to clarify their success. This is known as **"external with an internal check"**. And some communicators will sit in the middle of the continuum, possessing an **equal need to check internally and externally.**

When asked, *How do you know you are doing a good job?* someone with an **"internal feedback filter with an external check"** will say:
I just know, I get a good feeling and my team tell me.
Firstly, I had a good feeling we were doing well, then the figures verified this.
I felt like I was on track, then I looked at my competitors and saw I was in the lead.

When asked, *How do you know you are doing a good job?* someone with an **"external feedback filter with an internal check"** will answer:
My team thanks me, my manager says great work and then I just know.
Mainly I looked at the figures, but I also felt good about my achievements.
Firstly, I could see I was winning, and then it felt like I was heading in the right direction.

When asked, *How do you know you are doing a good job?* someone with an equal **"external"** and **"internal"** feedback filter" will reply:

I looked at the figures, but I also felt good about my achievements.
My team thanks me and I just know.
I could see I was winning, and it also felt like I was heading in the right direction.

Effective managers, coaches and leaders possess (or have learned) **an <u>internal</u> feedback filter with an <u>external</u> check**. They first go within to see, hear, grasp and process the effectiveness of their performance. Then they check outside of themselves for clarification. If the two checks vary significantly, **they will always trust or give more credence to the internal.** Why? Because they know the external may be fleeting, or susceptible to variables. It could be specific to the quirks of a particular group of people, and may never occur again. An external event may have artificially altered circumstances, yet this will not last.

An effective manager knows that whilst they design and bend their communication and decisions to their team's needs, they do not need to alter something which is working effectively for the majority of the time.

Someone with a highly internal feedback filter, takes instructions as suggestions. So, it is worth framing your requests as a suggestion, '*I suggest you have this report into me by 5pm today.* They will hear an instruction at a subconscious level and more likely to follow it up.

Someone with a highly external feedback filter, cares what other people think so they are interested in the research and studies which back up your advice. It is worth mentioning to them valid research and information e.g *'Research has shown that...'* or *'Many people have found that...'*

secret metaprogram 4: Talk to me

The fourth filter is called the **"speaking filter"**. It is how you prefer to give other people information, how you want them to talk to you and deliver spoken data.

When communicating, some people prefer to "give it to them straight", to "be direct" to "get to the point" This is known as a "**direct** speaking filter".

Other people prefer to deliver their information via a story, a metaphor, or an inference They expect you to "read between the lines". This is an "**inferential** speaking filter".

Both of these speaking styles have value. Their value depends on the listening and circumstances and the intent of the communication.

how using this filter helped us

Carol has a friend called Jana who is a direct communicator. Her background is in politics. When she communicates, Jana, gets straight to the point. Her communication is blunt and direct, sometimes bordering on harsh. She does not soften her words, nor prepare the listener for "bad" news.

When Carol first encountered Jana, she found her behaviour offensive, bordering on rude. Carol also observed Jana offending other people within their social circle. If she did not like what someone was wearing she would tell them. If she found a food not to her taste at a dinner party, she would inform the host. Often, she did not receive a second invitation. When Carol considered Jana, particularly in the context of her job, she quickly identified her as a "direct speaker".

She asked Jana about her role and what she did day to day. As she listened, she observed that Jana had no time for rhetoric or metaphor. She had to get to the point and get there quickly. She had achieved some extraordinary change in her community through being able to do this, change which someone with a less direct approach would never have accomplished.

Her speaking style was perfectly suited to her position, yet when transferred into social situations, it placed her out of rapport with those who preferred a softer, less direct approach. Knowing about metaprograms, meant Carol was able to see beyond Jana's "bluntness" or "rudeness" to the person she is. It also gave Carol the language to use when informing Jana that she had offended her.

how using this filter helped others

Scott, one of our clients, learned this information during our seminar. He realised his boss was an inferential or indirect speaker and it was driving him crazy! When needing to verify facts, he would have to sit through her regaling of lengthy stories, stories which may or may not have contained the data he needed. Learning about this metaprogram, gave him the skills to elicit the data he needed quickly and efficiently so he could get on with his job.

how using this filter helps you

Using the speaking style filter gives you the skills to get what you need when you need it. There are times for direct communication and other times more appropriate to indirect communication. Confident communicators know how to use the correct speaking style, and they when to use it.

how to elicit the speaking style filter

To elicit someone's preference for speaking style filter, ask them the following question:

If you have information or feedback for someone, would you prefer to tell them directly or give them the context or story behind the information?

Someone with a *"direct"* **speaking style filter** will answer:
I prefer to get straight to the point!
I just want to give them the data, so they can apply it.
I only have time to give them the facts, not the whole background or story.

Often, they are aware they come across as "blunt" or "too direct", and that their communication preference places them out of rapport with others. They may not know what to do to solve this. You can help them by asking them to "cut to the chase" and "give the main information". When you do this, you may receive a look of gratitude. This is because you have placed yourself in rapport with them and demonstrated you understand their model of the world.

Someone with an *"inferential"* **speaking style filter** will say:
They need the background, so they can put it in context.
I like to give my information in story-form. It's more fun that way.
Giving them a story about how I used this, helps them remember it.

If you have ever consulted a lawyer, you will have experienced a **direct speaking style** in action. Kathryn experienced anxiety when she sought the advice of a lawyer. What for her was a situation filled with strong emotion, and sensitive feelings, in which the story behind the details was important, was reduced to a series of harsh facts, and only those which could be proven via documentation. When she analysed it later, Kathryn found that understanding how an **indirect** speaking style had no place within that specific legal circumstance, helped soften the emotional blow.

To communicate effectively with a *"**direct**"* **speaker, it is best to:**
- ✓ Get to the point, and quickly e.g *I've called you in here to discuss your performance in the last competition.*

- ✓ Only give them the necessary data e.g *Here are the figures for the June quarter.*
- ✓ Summarise briefly if a context is required, so they only receive what they need
- ✓ Avoid long and unnecessary stories they don't need or want them

To communicate effectively with an **"*indirect*"** **speaker, it is best to:**
- ✓ Give them a background context before you deliver the key information e.g *Do you remember how we agreed to hold regular performance reviews? Last time we discussed the need for you to... so I've called you in here to discuss your performance in the last competition.*
- ✓ Deliver the information via a story or metaphor e.g *Remember Jenny who used to work here? I spoke with her the other day and she told me about her experiences with the team in Barcelona...*
- ✓ Give the context for your discussion or information; lead into it
- ✓ Give them stories or metaphor—it gives them a context to process the information

secret metaprogram 5: I'm listening

This next filter is called the **"listening filter"**. It is how you prefer other people to talk to you, and how you want them to deliver spoken data. It is how you receive the information people give you. It's how you prefer they communicate with you: directly or indirectly, inferentially or factually.

Some people prefer you to get straight to the point, give them the facts, cut to the chase. We call this a **"direct"** listener.

Other people prefer you to communicate indirectly, gently, using euphemism or gesture. We call this an "**indirect**" listener.

how using this filter helped us

Kathryn had a CEO who was an indirect communicator. He loved telling stories to make a point. The problem was, his stories went on for a long time and, after having gleaned the point of his message, Kathryn would politely sit through another ten minutes of metaphor, frustrated because she had work to get on with. If he was delivering "bad news", she would feel sick in the gut as she sensed the information coming.

When she learned this information, she was able to explain to him their differences and how his speaking style impacted on her listening preference. From then on, he only delivered her the key facts she required to move on with her job. If he had to deliver "bad news" he thought she might not enjoy hearing, he got straight to the point which she appreciated. When they socialised out of work hours, she happily listened to his stories, understanding his need to tell them.

how using this filter helped others

Nicole's coach, Jenna, was a direct speaker. Nicole, on the other hand, is an indirect listener. Before a race, her coach would pull her aside, giving her direct and specific directions on each stage of her swim. Nicole would go into overwhelm with all the information coming at her. She also found Jenna's manner abrupt and upsetting. It distracted her from giving her best performance.

When Nicole heard this information, she spoke to Jenna at the end of a training session. After ensuring their body language was in rapport–Nicole is an excellent student and a fast learner–Nicole explained what she had learned and how she needed to be communicated with in a less direct manner. She respectfully asked if Jenna would be able to do this. Wanting the best from her athlete, Jenna happily complied. Now, before a race, Jenna reminds Nicole of another time she achieved success. This inspires Nicole in the way she needs, and she is happy to report her PB has improved significantly.

how using this filter helps you

Applying the listening filter in a way someone else needs, is akin to speaking *their* language. Just as you speak English to an English speaker, and visual language to a visual communicator, speaking directly as someone needs it gains and maintains rapport. Good rapport equals good communication.

how to elicit the listening style filter

To elicit someone's _**listening**_ style filter, ask them the following question: ***If I have information or feedback for you, would you prefer to hear it directly, or do you require the context or story behind the information?***

Someone with a _"direct"_ listening style filter will answer:
I want you to get to the point! Please!
I do not need the whole saga; I just want to hear the facts.
I don't see the point of a whole story.
When someone goes on and on and on, I find it annoying, frustrating and I find them "boring" or "fluffy".

Someone with an _"inferential"_ listening style filter will say:
Hearing a story about how you used this, helps me remember it better.
I need the background, so I can put it in context.
I like to hear information in story-form. It's more fun that way.
When someone gets to the point too quickly, or are too direct, I find them rude.

To communicate effectively with a *"direct"* listener, it is best to:
- ✓ Get to the point, and quickly e.g *I've called you in here to discuss your performance in the last competition.*
- ✓ Ensure your facts are correct and current; they don't appreciate having their time wasted with unnecessary data
- ✓ Only give them the necessary data e.g *Here are the figures for the June quarter.*
- ✓ Summarise briefly if a context is required, so they only receive what they need
- ✓ Avoid long and unnecessary stories, they don't need or want them, and they become annoyed by them, thus placing you out of rapport

To communicate effectively with an *"indirect"* listener, it is best to:
- ✓ Give them a background context before you deliver the key information e.g *Do you remember how we agreed to hold monthly planning meetings? Last time we discussed the need for you to...so I've called you in here to receive the data you gathered.*
- ✓ Deliver the information via a story or metaphor e.g *Remember John who used to work here? He had a similar situation in Rio and here's how he solved it.*
- ✓ Give the context for your discussion or information
- ✓ Be sensitive to their feelings and how the information may impact them. Lead into it; warm

them up, especially if the information is "sensitive" or emotional in content
- ✓ Give them relevant success stories, it gives them a context to process the information
- ✓ Avoid gossip–they are extremely sensitive to it, and may even interpret that you are giving them a metaphor for something they need to change about themselves

It is worth noting that **not all direct speakers are direct listeners.** And **not all indirect speakers are indirect listeners.** We cannot easily predict this, so it is faster and simpler to ask someone how they wish to be communicated with. Most people appreciate this as they identify your efforts to increase rapport and gain effective communication.

Kathryn is an "*indirect listener*", yet she **prefers someone to speak directly with her** and get to the point. Hearing someone "waffle on" annoys her; she considers it a time waster, particularly in a business environment. As a kinesthetic, she can sense when someone is delivering "bad" news, and it makes her feel sick to the stomach. She needs the speaker to get to the point faster, so she can process the information, particularly on an emotional level.

Carol is a "*direct speaker*". Prior to learning this information, she could not see the point of someone telling stories in any context apart from at a dinner party. She had to learn to include metaphor in her presentations. She embraced this so effectively, she developed a whole technique around it.

chapter 20   body language bonus – the confidence stance

Whilst it is vital to mirror someone's body language, thus placing yourself in rapport, it is also important and appropriate to have a way of communicating your confidence. In our world, there are several universal gestures or stances which communicate specific messages. The "thumbs up" gesture is an example of this. The "peace sign" is another one.

A few years ago, an opera singer friend of Carol's taught her the "confidence stance". It is a gesture which communicates your value. It says:

I am confident.

I am wise

I am approachable

I am centred.

I am intelligent.

I am calm and composed.

I know myself well.

What I say is of equal value to what you have to say.

I am an excellent listener.

I am a clear and centred communicator.

All this is communicated with a single gesture!

how the confidence stance helps us

Carol uses the confidence stance when she is presenting to large groups. She begins using the gesture while standing to the side of the stage as she is introduced, thus already communicating her confidence to her audience. It works on two levels. It grounds and centres her, preparing her to deliver a clear and dynamic presentation.

Secondly, it helps her appear confident to others. It boosts the receptiveness of the message she is delivering. Studies have shown we pay more attention to people we perceive as confident. We value their opinion more. We accept their information. Using the confidence stance eliminates the pre-judging which may occur even before Carol has said a single word.

the confidence stance works on two levels

1. How you feel: It is a grounding stance which centres you. It helps you prepare for your performance, whether it is one-on-one, a small group, a board meeting or a large audience. It places you in the right mindset for effective and clear communication.

2. How you are perceived: the confidence stance helps you emit an energy of clarity and, well, confidence. This makes other people more interested in what you have to say, show them and give them.

how the confidence stance helped others

Colleen learned the communication stance at one of Carol's Confident Communication Masterclasses. She excitedly reported back her achievements.

'I've been chairing this board for a year, and been frustrated with certain members not listening to me or taking me seriously. Sometimes, things become so chaotic, I've considered bringing in a bell, to ring and call people's attention back to the agenda.

Last week, after learning the "confidence stance", I used the stance during our monthly meeting. People were actually listening to me!

At one point, debate was becoming heated, and I had something important to say. Remaining silent, I consciously adopted the seated communication stance. Like magic, one-by-one, people stopped talking, turned to me, and waited for me to speak. I had not said a word. But I had communicated volumes!

I love this communication stance. I'm going to use it at a networking function tomorrow. For the first time in many years, I am actually excited about attending!'

During an executive coaching session, Natalie confessed to Carol that she was nervous about networking. She even said she hated it with a passion. She had a huge function coming up in which several key players in her industry would be in attendance. She wanted to make a good impression.

Carol showed her the communication stance. Natalie excitedly applied it, enabling her to gain and maintain rapport with key people who can assist her in moving into a new role. She no longer "hates" networking, instead telling Carol it is 'fun and easy!'

when do I use the confidence stance?

You can use the confidence stance to empower yourself in the following situations:

- ✓ networking
- ✓ meetings
- ✓ chairing a board
- ✓ sales pitches
- ✓ presenting, teaching or training
- ✓ media
- ✓ job interviews
- ✓ managing others
- ✓ facilitating a panel
- ✓ potential conflict situations

how to "do" the confidence stance

The confidence stance is as follows:

- ✓ Stand, with both feet planted firmly on the ground
- ✓ Place feet hip-width apart
- ✓ slight bend in the knee
- ✓ hand grasping opposite wrist where your watch would be.

you can even do the confidence stance when sitting

The *seated* "confidence stance" is as follows:

- ✓ Seated, with both feet planted firmly on the ground
- ✓ Legs uncrossed
- ✓ hand grasping opposite wrist where your watch would be. and placed in your lap or on the table in front of you

When wearing a skirt or dress, be aware of what is on display! With knees pressed together, tilt your knees slightly to one side, feet on the floor. Modern boardroom tables are sometimes clear glass, so again, be aware of what you are communicating from the waist down.

Our shorter-legged clients, whose feet do not generally touch the ground when seated, have found it helpful to shift forward in their seat, so feet are planted firmly on the ground. This grounds them, and assists in radiating confidence.

during a one-on-one conversation, do I "mirror" someone, or use the "confidence stance"?

Both. In a situation requiring confident communication, you could begin with a confidence stance, then mirror the other person. This is useful if you want to convey immediate confidence, particularly if they hold a high-profile role and you want to meet them as an equal.

If you want instant rapport, mirror their body language, then shift to the communication stance. **You may notice them follow you, changing their gestures as you do.** In psychology, this is referred to as **"leading and pacing"**. It shows if someone is in rapport with you. If they change their body language to follow yours, you have made a connection.

If they don't follow your lead, mirror them for a little longer, then shift again to the confidence stance. Some people simply need more time to "warm up".

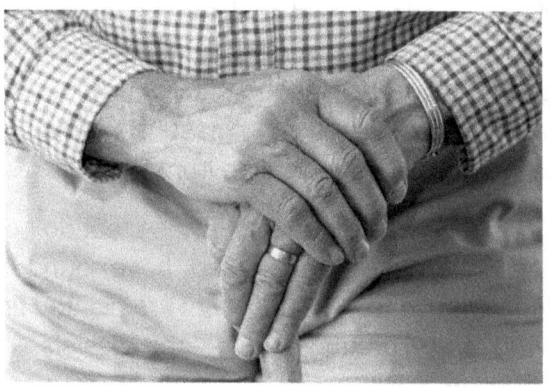

In the above image, when you look carefully you can see this man is holding a walking stick. When we first saw this image, it struck us how similar it appeared to a confidence stance, and how, when we see someone standing this way they appear confident. We may even refer to them as "dapper". When they begin to walk, on shaky legs however, they communicate something different. Yet, while they stand tall, balancing on their stick, they communicate confidence.

chapter 21 how to be a confident communicator in your world

Our aim for this book was to share information in a way that is practical, simple and quick to apply. One of the easiest ways to apply this information is to give yourself a conscious focus for one week, e.g: mirroring body language, email rapport, mirroring voice tone or volume, and to apply this in all your interactions. It then becomes automatic for you to do this at a subconscious mind level.

You will do this when you are very clear now on the reasons *why* you would want to become a confident communicator.

These reasons might include:
- ✓ attracting and maintaining fulfilling personal and business relationships
- ✓ increasing opportunities e.g promotions, payrises, networking
- ✓ more effective management and coaching
- ✓ improved public speaking skills
- ✓ avoiding poor communication
- ✓ creating and maintaining a happy home
- ✓ averting "drama" at work or at home
- ✓ having a harmonious workplace

As you see, hear and become clear now on your personal motivations for confident communication, take the data, vision and suggestions throughout this book and apply them in your life.

we enjoy seeing, hearing and receiving feedback on how our readers use this information

We love constructive feedback. If you see, hear or deem this information of value, and want to share your wins and stories with us, please post a message on our Facebook page **carolfox.confidentcommunication** or email us at **info@carolfox.com.au**

bibliography
Birdwhistell, Ray L. Kinesics and Context. Philadelphia: University of Pennsylvania Press, 1970

Csikszentmihalyi, Mihaly. Flow: The Psychology of Optimal Experience. New York: Harper and Row, 1990

James, Tad & Woodsmall, Wyatt, *Time Line Therapy and the Basis of Personality*, Crown House Publishing Ltd, 2017)

suggested reading
These are a series of references we have found particularly useful, in terms of communication and general personal development. Enjoy checking them out!

The Mind Map Book: How to Use Radiant Thinking to Maximize Your Brain's Untapped Potential by Tony Buzan, with Barry Buzan

Ageless Body, Timeless Mind by Deepak Chopra, M.D.,

Creating Affluence: Wealth Consciousness in the Field of all Possibilities by Deepak Chopra, M.D.,

In Search of Excellence by Thomas J. Peters, Robert H. Waterman, Jr.

The Alchemist by Paulo Coelho

Awaken the Giant Within by Anthony Robbins

Frogs into Princes by Richard Bandler & John Grinder

Handbook of Hypnotic Suggestion & Metaphor by D. Corydon Hammond

Kinesics and Context by Ray L. Birdwhistle

The Magic of NLP Demystified by Byron Lewis & Frank Pucelik

Rich Dad, Poor Dad by Robert Kiyosaki

The Teaching Tales of Milton Erickson by Ernest L. Rossi

Therapeutic Metaphors by David Gordon

The Holographic Universe by Michael Talbot

What the Bleep Do We Know- Discovering The Endless Possibilities for Altering Your Everyday Reality by William Arntz, Betsy Chasse and Mark Vicente

confident communication programs
- Would you like change in your workplace?
- Would you like to avoid poor communication and replace it with confidence?
- Would you like all your team to see, hear, receive and learn this information?

At *Carol Fox - Confident Communication for Leaders*, we offer bespoke workshops, masterclasses and keynote presentations on this and other topics, tailored specifically to your needs. Visit www.carolfox.com.au for more information on the variety of teams we work with.

do it on purpose – live your values
- ✓ Identify what your team values
- ✓ Build your team
- ✓ Develop behavioural codes
- ✓ If you're going to do it - do it on purpose.

replace can't – identify your stories
- ✓ Recognize your negative stories
- ✓ Replace blame with responsibility
- ✓ Remove beliefs that limit your success
- ✓ Empower yourself – replace can't.

disconnect the hot buttons – dealing with conflict
- ✓ You can disconnect your hot buttons
- ✓ 'Reframing' takes the heat out of a situation
- ✓ Positive self-talk creates a positive reality
- ✓ It's not about you so - disconnect the hot buttons

walk their talk – communicate with confidence
- ✓ Use words that hit the mark
- ✓ Create and maintain exceptional relationships
- ✓ Build a team that knows how best to work together
- ✓ Communicate with confidence – walk their talk

imagine a new reality – goal setting for excellence
- ✓ Identify your goals
- ✓ Discover what beliefs hold you back
- ✓ Pinpoint the exact moment you achieve your goal
- ✓ Celebrate your achievements – imagine a new reality

talk yourself into it – the power of words
- ✓ Use words that motivate and empower
- ✓ Focus on what you want
- ✓ Rephrase to maximize impact
- ✓ Whatever your desired outcome – talk yourself into it

demystify dick and dora – men and women are different
- ✓ How men and women are different
- ✓ Why hormones play a role for both genders
- ✓ Effective communication strategies for both genders
- ✓ Communicate effectively - Demystify Dick and Dora

no-pill chill skills – stress management strategies
- ✓ Eliminate anxiety leading up to previously stressful events
- ✓ Put yourself into a calmer state – anywhere, anytime

- ✓ Reinforce your goal with visualization and positive self-talk
- ✓ Respond with confidence and clarity with - No-pill chill skills

get cued in – learn to influence
- ✓ Identify what motivates people
- ✓ Influence people using their motivators
- ✓ Create win-win situations for increased achievement
- ✓ Learn to influence – get cued in

present to sizzle – advanced presenting skills
- ✓ Create instant connections
- ✓ Understand the four different communication styles
- ✓ Speak the language of all members of your audience
- ✓ Engage your audience - present to sizzle

you can make time – time management
- ✓ Eliminate procrastination
- ✓ Improve your focus
- ✓ Increase your productivity
- ✓ Embrace life's challenges because – you can make time

For more information contact us:
www.carolfox.com.au
Phone: 1800 790 599
Email: info@carolfox.com.au

about the authors

Carol Fox: After thirty years in the personal and professional development arena, Carol is like a personal GPS for leaders. She has taught thousands of people to communicate with confidence in their professional and personal lives. Carol is currently the chair of Women Sport Australia, the peak national not-for-profit organisation providing leadership to women and girls in sport. Through her company's masterclasses, workshops, executive coaching and key-note speaking, she continues to offer leaders the most effective, cutting-edge-techniques for ultimate confident communication.

Kathryn Gorman worked in education for over a decade, where she thrilled at seeing her students crack the code of communication and learn to read and write. She has lectured in communication skills at a university level, and was the national training manager for an accelerated learning organisation. For over fifteen years she worked as a hypnotherapist and corporate trainer. Kathryn enjoys discovering, utilising and writing about fast, simple solutions for effective and permanent change. She now writes full time.

Confident Communication for Leaders

www.ingramcontent.com/pod-product-compliance
Lightning Source LLC
Chambersburg PA
CBHW070738160426
43192CB00009B/1493